SONS AND *Mothers*

SONS AND *Mothers*
STORIES FROM MENNONITE MEN

edited by Mary Ann Loewen

University of Regina Press

© 2015 Mary Ann Loewen

All rights reserved. No part of this work covered by the copyrights hereon may be reproduced or used in any form or by any means—graphic, electronic, or mechanical—without the prior written permission of the publisher. Any request for photocopying, recording, taping or placement in information storage and retrieval systems of any sort shall be directed in writing to Access Copyright.

Printed and bound in Canada at Webcom.
Cover and text design: Duncan Campbell, University of Regina Press
Copy editor: Anne James
Proofreader: Kristine Douaud
Cover photo: "Retro / Vintage Apron" by Susanne Alfredsson / Snapwire.

Library and Archives Canada Cataloguing in Publication
Sons and mothers : stories from Mennonite men / edited
by Mary Ann Loewen.

Issued in print and electronic formats.
ISBN 978-0-88977-403-2 (paperback).—ISBN 978-0-88977-406-3 (html).
—ISBN 978-0-88977-405-6 (pdf)

1. Mennonite women—Canada. 2. Motherhood—Religious aspects—Mennonites. 3. Mennonites—Family relationships—Canada. 4. Mothers and sons—Canada. I. Loewen, Mary Ann, 1956-, editor

BX8128.W64S65 2015   305.48'6897   C2015-903834-0   C2015-903835-9

10 9 8 7 6 5 4 3 2 1

University of Regina Press, University of Regina
Regina, Saskatchewan, Canada, S4S 0A2
tel: (306) 585-4758 fax: (306) 585-4699
web: www.uofrpress.ca

We acknowledge the financial support of the Government of Canada through the Canada Book Fund for our publishing activities. We acknowledge the support of the Canada Council for the Arts for our publishing program. This publication was made possible through Creative Saskatchewan's Creative Industries Production Grant Program.

This book is dedicated first to the men who give us their mothers as children, as wives, as girlfriends, as parents, as women. As stalwart Christians, as vulnerable migrants, as disease-ridden seniors, as reluctant rebels, as trendy fashionistas, as vicarious musicians, as caring nurturers, as open-minded supporters, as women who "do not go gentle into that good night." Thank you, men, for your honest stories.

And second, it is dedicated to all mothers, who are both bulwarks and fascinating, many-faceted, non-stereotypical human beings.

CONTENTS

Introduction—*Mary Ann Loewen* ix

Things My Friends Did Not Know
    about My Mom—*Paul Tiessen* 1

Rituals, Rhythms, and
    Memories of My Mother—*John Rempel* 15

Gifts from My Mother—*Josiah Neufeld* 31

Open Gates—*Nathan Klippenstein* 41

Fifteen Ways to a More Beautiful You—*Byron Rempel* 57

Happiness in the Face of Austerity, Boredom,
    and Strict Morality: A Discussion between
    Mennonite Mothers and Their Sons about Dating
    —*Lukas Thiessen* 73

"heritage"—*Christoff Engbrecht* 85

Mary Dyck's Vicarious Life—*Howard Dyck* 89

Reconciling Caring with Conflict:
    A Memoir of Mom—*Andrew C. Martin* 99

Queen of Clubs—*Lloyd Ratzlaff* 113

Malaver
    Two Poems
    —*Michael Goertzen* 119

I Give a Rip—*Patrick Friesen* 129

Contributors 141

Introduction

Mary Ann Loewen

Every culture has its way of telling a story. Every culture has its notion of what a family is, what a mother and a father are. This collection represents stories and poems written by men about their mothers, and although these men write about their Mennonite mothers, anyone who opens this book will come to understand that although a particular culture offers a certain way of seeing life, for all of us "our life stories are not merely *about* us but in an inescapable and profound way *are* us" (John Paul Eakin, x). This anthology is a set of narratives about the significant mother-son relationship and, as such, has to do with the identities of both the son and the mother.

In their introduction to *Mothering Mennonite*, a collection of essays in which women write about their Mennonite mothers, editors Rachel Epp Buller and Kerry Fast suggest that "various directions for future research on Mennonite mothering remain open" (14). During the Q&A of the Winnipeg book launch of this ambitious, imaginative, and successful collection in June of 2013, a variety of questions were asked, but one in particular caught my ear: "We see that women have had a chance to write about their experience as daughters of Mennonite mothers, but have men had a similar opportunity?" The answer, as far as the editors knew, was no. So that evening I decided to take up the challenge of crossing the gender/generation divide and allow men to share their stories about their Mennonite mothers. I decided to become the "coaxer," to use a term coined by Ken Plummer, soliciting stories from these men (21).

Indeed, Buller and Fast's encouragement to keep exploring the area of mothering is an incentive to think outside of the familiar gender box. To consider that not only women, as Virginia Woolf suggests, "think back through their mothers" (88), but that perhaps men do, too. And clearly they do, if the enthusiasm from the writers I approached to be a part of this project is any indication.

This anthology includes both prose and poetry, in which male writers share their memories—both good and bad, happy and sad, ordinary and profound—of their mother-son relationships. The pieces evoke a variety of occasions: conversations—both casual and momentous; significant historical events—both pleasurable and traumatic; remembered moments—both tender and harsh; and experiences—both quotidian and life-changing. The looking back affords the contributor an opportunity to observe his mother as both a woman and a mother, and to consider his life as a son; to remember when his mother understood him, and when she did not; to recall occasions when time stood still, so magical was the mother-son moment; to realize how proud his mother was/is of him; to reflect upon how his mother has impacted him as a son, a friend, a father, a wage-earner, a professional, a husband, a grandfather.

As the writer writes, his story *becomes*; memories beget memories; stories beget stories. Certainly the perception of what has transpired years ago shifts over time. As Judith Summerfield affirms, "There is no return to the event, except 'virtually'" (185), and of course all writers "play *at* and *with* subject positions" (Spigelman, italics mine, 126). But that is not to say that the stories here are not true. In fact, I suggest the very opposite. I strongly believe that sentiment and memory are as valuable—if not more so—to a memoir, as are the facts, and I agree with Smith and Watson who maintain that reducing "autobiographical narration to facticity ... strip[s] it of the densities of rhetorical, literary, ethical, political, and cultural dimensions" (13). Surely *the act of remembering* deepens the original experience, for over time the story takes on a meaning that was not possible at the time of the specific event, the particular occasion; the story gradually unfolds itself as it becomes a part of a life's (indeed, a son's) greater narrative.

Asking men to write about their mothers is a potentially controversial undertaking, both because men and women represent different genders and because a good portion of the narrative could be seen as a kind of appropriation of another's voice. The past few decades have seen women write for themselves, about themselves, and finding within that action an agency they had not previously been privy to; is it then politically correct to give the "driver's seat" back to the men? And what about appropriation: Can a white person write authoritatively about an Aboriginal person? Can a heterosexual write knowingly about a gay man? Can a woman who has not had a child write convincingly from the viewpoint of a mother? And to the point, can men, who are both male and unable to bear children, write justifiable stories about females who have borne children? My answer to all of these questions is yes. So, in fact, it is not only *politically correct* to allow men to tell stories about women; it is imperative that both genders tell their life stories, for only when women and men work together is the gender divide likely to dissolve. And yes, it is okay for men to write about their mothers because what makes these particular narratives legitimate is that they are written from the sons' perspectives; although they relate stories about their mothers, both the memories and the voices are inherently their own.

We tell our stories in order to make sense of our lives, and we read the stories of others in order to know and understand what it is to be human, what it is to struggle, to love, to weep, to laugh, to rejoice, to grieve. Certainly "that magical opportunity of entering another life is what really sets us thinking about our own" (Ker Conway, n.p.). Indeed, writers and readers need each other if stories are to make a difference in our lives, for it is within that particular exchange that truth "outs" itself, that a shared understanding begins to emerge.

Every ethnicity has its particular way of calling the past to mind. Certainly Mennonites, as a community, "develop their own occasions, rituals, archives, and practices of remembering" (Smith and Watson, 25), and certainly the culture of Mennonites plays into this collection in a significant way. From young men surprised by incorrect assumptions about the Mennonite church they grew up in, to older men realizing the momentousness of a mother who stayed home from her Mennonite church on a Sunday morning—this specific culture dictated a certain code of behaviour within each of its distinct communities. And so when a young woman chooses to bypass these presuppositions, there is a story. But when a young woman chooses to abide by these assumptions, there is still a story. And when a mother experiences conflict between the community's assumptions and her natural bents, the story is fascinating. Both the "sons" who write these stories and the sons and daughters reading them identify with some kind of cultural setting. And while this particular collection chooses as its focus the Mennonite tradition, regardless of the specific custom, for all of us story and remembering are ways to recognize our shared human experience. And so, just as Miriam Toews' *A Complicated Kindness* (2004) found resonance in the hearts of young women of all kinds of ethnic and religious backgrounds through the narration of its protagonist, Nomi, so too these stories will move not just the Mennonite "child," but also the Muslim, the Jew, the atheist, and the agnostic, the Catholic, as well as the secularist, child. We are all children born of mothers, and all of us seek to understand one another in an attempt to make sense of our own lives.

In the past decades, life writing has gone through various stages. While perhaps as recently as twenty years ago "autobiography consolidated its status as a ... discourse that served to power and define centers, margins, boundaries, and grounds of action in the West" (Smith, 18), today personal narrative and/or memoir is seen as an undertaking that seeks to recognize the ordinary person, that looks to understand the importance of the everyday life. Thus life writing is recognized as legitimate in the academic world because, as Richard Miller points out, "all intellectual projects are always, inevitably, also autobiographies" (50), but it is also recognized more generally for its role in helping us sort out our individual and collective identities, our past and our present lives. Thus life writing has, in essence, become necessary.

A variety of fairly specific threads are probed in this collection. The Russian revolution of 1917 and its lasting psychological effects are crucial to several contributions. As Paul Tiessen talks lovingly about his mother, he discloses her intentional absence from the institution of church in her early forties, an absence quite possibly due to traumas experienced in Russia. John Rempel recounts how his mother's firsthand experience with the anarchy of Machno and his henchmen resulted in an insistence on daily, monthly, and even yearly rhythms to family life in Canada—as a way of slaying demons and exerting a modicum of control in a world of uncertainty. These narratives suggest that the sudden, traumatic events in Russia shattered the women's assumed protected and secure lives, and resulted in repression, in an incumbent inability to share their pasts with others. Although they managed to create a safe and economically sound life for themselves here in Canada, their difficult history remained a part of who they were. And as Susan Brison argues, "attempting to limit traumatic memories does not make them go away; the signs and symptoms of trauma remain, caused by a source more virulent for being driven underground" (58).

Also examined is the spiritual fervour of mothers who believed they were doing the right thing by insisting on strict religious devotion. These mothers' evangelical zeal—though sincere and positively motivated—often left the sons feeling stifled, lost, and sometimes confused. Josiah Neufeld's difficult conversations with his mother about his choice to take his wife's surname reflect his and his mother's polarizing views on gender roles; Nathan Klippenstein's descriptions of countless mandatory prayers of penitence reveal both his inability to "measure up," and a religion plagued by judgment; and Byron Rempel's poetic unveiling of his mother's worldly priorities exposes a faith afraid of what is on the inside. The sons' eventual responses to these influences were to leave the religious path of their mothers to explore a faith, a way of being in the world, that allowed them to be true to who they were, to who they were becoming.

In contrast to the conservative, evangelical mother is the less traditional mother. In the case of Lukas Thiessen, it is a mother who not only allows her son the freedom to experiment with "worldly" practices, but also freely acknowledges her own earlier exploration in matters such as dating and sexuality. Thiessen's interviews with his peers and their mothers are both surprising and revealing. While the age of the mothers may partially account for their openness, their answers are nonetheless enlightening and serve to build bridges between the generations. And Christoff Engbrecht's contribution, the poem "*heritage*" offers a unique perspective: while his father is Mennonite, his mother is Irish. This conflation of faith traditions, combined with a common interest in poetry, makes for an unusual mother-son relationship.

The response to a lack of educational opportunity, of exposure to ideas taught in institutions of higher learning (perhaps related to the patriarchal underpinnings of the Mennonite faith, particularly fifty years ago) is also examined in this collection. Howard Dyck writes of his close connection to his mother through a common love of music; his achievements in the professional world of choral conducting were lauded and experienced vicariously by his mother, who silently rued her own lack of education and opportunity. And Andrew C. Martin poignantly works through his difficult past as he describes a life of passive-aggressive role modelling, an inability on his mother's part to work through conflict in a constructive way due to a restrictive social environment.

Several authors speak of the difficulty in seeing their mothers become not only dependent, but significantly changed, when illness and/or old age exacts its toll. Lloyd Ratzlaff offers a moving account of his mother's losing battle with a sudden case of meningitis at age eighty-five, and Nathan Klippenstein recalls his mother's tortured attempts to speak after a brutal stroke betrays her once alert and intelligent mind. Michael Goertzen shares the effects of his mother's cancer and its treatment as he simultaneously tries to make sense of his relationship with her. Patrick Friesen shares the agony of having to break the news to his mother—a woman who chose "a romantic fram[e]" for her life—that her independent days are over, that it is time to move into a care home.

Woven through these stories of frustration, of loss, of gradual or sudden understanding, of heartbreak, of tenderness, of celebration, of everyday events is a thread that speaks of a gentle, adult awareness of what a mother has meant to a son. An awareness, too, of mother as child, mother as young woman, mother as writer and gardener and spouse and nurse and chorister and seamstress and patient and sibling and lover and church member. Mother with interests and loves and insecurities and disappointments and talents and inabilities and strengths and weaknesses. Mother as human being.

What to make of a mother who has to have her hair done, even on her deathbed? What to make of a mother who insists on one more church service when all of her children are overtired and enormously hungry? What to make of a mother who suddenly stops going to church in mid-life? What to make of a mother who recycles long before it is cool to do so? What to make of a mother who is kind and gentle one minute and fierce and angry the next? What to make of a mother who dislikes her husband? What to make of a mother who has the "trickster" in her? What to make of a mother who laments the lack of education and lives vicariously through her son's accomplishments? What to make of a mother whose eye leaks because of cancer treatment? What to make of mothers who love their sons unconditionally?

These contributors "make of" their mothers what their mothers tell them in person, or posthumously, what they tell them with their voices and, more importantly, with their spirits. Mostly these sons make of their mothers through their own memories, through their own eyes. They create, re-create their mothers, and their intense, difficult, easygoing, and beautiful relationships with these women. Everyone has a story. Everyone has a mother. Here are a few stories of sons and mothers.

Works Cited

Brison, Susan. *Aftermath: Violence and the Remaking of a Self.* Princeton: Princeton University Press, 2002.

Buller, Rachel Epp, and Kerry Fast, eds. *Mothering Mennonite.* Bradford: Demeter Press, 2013.

Conway, Jill Ker. *When Memory Speaks: Reflections on Autobiography.* New York: Alfred A. Knopf, 1998.

Eakin, John Paul. *Living Autobiographically: How we Create Identity in Narrative.* Ithaca: Cornell University Press, 2008.

Miller, Richard. *Writing at the End of the World.* Pittsburgh: University of Pittsburgh Press, 2005.

Plummer, Ken. *Telling Sexual Stories: Power, Change and Social Worlds.* London: Routledge, 1995.

Smith, Sidonie. *Subjectivity, Identity, and the Body.* Bloomington: Indiana University Press, 1993.

Smith, Sidonie, and Julia Watson. *Reading Autobiography: A Guide for Interpreting Life Narratives.* Minneapolis: University of Minnesota Press, 2010.

Spigelman, Candace. *Personally Speaking: Experience as Evidence in Academic Discourse.* Carbondale: Southern Illinois University Press, 2004.

Summerfield, Judith. "Is There a Life in This Text? Reimagining Narrative." In *Writing Theory and Critical Theory,* edited by John Clifford and John Schilb, 179–94. New York: Modern Language Association, 1994.

Woolf, Virgina. *A Room of One's Own.* London: Penguin Books, 1956.

Helen and Paul

Things My Friends Did Not Know about My Mom

Paul Tiessen

1.

One thing that my friends did not know about my mom, Helen (Reimer) Tiessen, was that in 1950, when she was forty-two and I was six, she became something of a social recluse. We had just moved to Kitchener and were starting to attend the big Kitchener Mennonite Brethren church. She did not withdraw from my dad or my sister or me, but—and over the years I started to think to myself that this was peculiar—she started to withdraw from the ongoing and vigorous activity of church life.

Another thing was this: as though to accompany her emerging diffidence within church circles, she and I began a more or less private conversational relationship that we kept going with increasing intensity for seventeen years, until 1967, when I moved away from home to go to graduate school. Especially as I grew older during my high school and on into my undergraduate years, we would pursue extraordinary late-night conversations, perhaps once a month, plus ordinary give-and-take everyday conversations. We were both nighthawks anyway, and she, as much as any two or three of my closest friends, became my confidante, at least at some level.

I always benefited from her endless forbearance and sweet gentleness and (though I did not know it at the time) her incredible experience of life. In the face of my critical impatience with certain church matters as I grew older, I sorted out a range of questions with her: about identity and ambition, family and relationships, sports and pop culture, church and religion. She helped me think about my life at the huge public elementary school that I entered in 1950, where I thrived—"with God's help," as my mom would ceaselessly remind me—in the hands of a series of excellent teachers. When she and I differed, she never tried to convince by argument; she simply endorsed the positive.

Simultaneously in 1950 she found a space outside our immediate family that was for her a stimulating and rewarding extension of our home, and one that served as an alternative to church attendance and involvement. She began visiting her own mom and her siblings, in a house right across the street from the church. My mom enjoyed her wise, gracious, and magnanimous mother, and her four unmarried siblings—a brother and three sisters—showing interest in their successes at jobs and, perhaps too frequently, their loss of jobs in the city, their illnesses and cures, their adventures and misadventures with friends, their encounters, both good and bad, in church life (where her one sister, Clara, sometimes sang solos).

With other relatives often visiting too, I spent many Sunday afternoons at that house, witnessing my mom and my dad among my aunts and uncles, cousins and grandma, engaging in spirited talk, playing piano, singing—and enjoying *zweibach* and much else that made up the wonderful spread that was *faspa*. My grandma's conversation kept up with everyone's and, to be sure, stimulated a wide-ranging view and astute observation of national and international political and religious situations. Indeed, my grandmother's perspective had developed broadly by the time she was twenty, because from 1902 to 1904 she worked as a seamstress in the estate household at Steinbach, Molotschna, regularly joining the community-minded Peter Schmidt and his family for meals and the conversations around the table there. With her worldly wise intelligence, my grandma—always showing interest in all of us—consistently gave my mom and others an optimistic yet pragmatic way of seeing and feeling the world. For example, one day during the 1940s she went to the Kitchener City Park to meet Prime Minister Mackenzie King on a visit to his hometown, to thank him face to face for his social policies involving family welfare, and his vigorous support for and high view of Mennonites. She energized many people who came for visits in her little house which, by the 1960s, due to failing health, she only infrequently left. And so she energized my mom, who visited that house almost daily.

For my mom, our church—lively and, by all appearances, very successful—was too much to put up with in terms of its social and psychological expectations. She seemed cowed by the apparent absolutes of its well-oiled social apparatus, its programmatic approval of presumed and, to be sure, occasionally enforced, behavioural normalcy, and its operating at full throttle on multiple fronts in the here and now. Certainly it had developed enormous strengths of its own over its twenty-five-year history that had run through the Depression and the Second World War. Perhaps, missing the "pioneering" spirit that gave energy to so many phases of her life before 1950, she found our church too settled in its ways, too established. While I found plenty of great people and lovely action there—from involvement in choirs, quartets, drama groups, study groups, committees, and charity work, to attending youth events, parties, banquets and guest lectures, and even a bus excursion to the Shaw theatre in Niagara-on-the-Lake—on Sunday mornings my mom simply stayed at my grandma's, where she could listen in to the church service through a closed-circuit hookup. And no one seemed to mind. My dad—a regular at church who loved its social and institutional life, and who held all kinds of attendant responsibilities—did not object. Members of the congregation also said nothing about her absence from most events. Meanwhile my friends' mothers (some of whom were part of the "village" of mothers involved in raising all of us kids) carried on in the church: confident and energetic, happy and assured.

I realize now that my mom could not see a role for herself in this church, after having for most of her forty-two years been a highly involved and even favoured participant with lots of connections at significant levels of previous church life. It may be that she sensed a sudden loss of position in 1950 when my dad—known by then as *Lehrer* Tiessen among Russian Mennonites in Ontario, having ended a high-profile job as founding principal of the Mennonite high school in the Niagara Peninsula—took on an ordinary and less visible position in a public elementary school near Kitchener. It may be that she lacked the support of her older and gregarious sister, Lydia, who had moved away from Kitchener with her husband just one year before, to work with the Mennonite Central Committee in Japan; had she been around in 1950, she could have made sure my mom was "connected." But by the time Aunt Lydia returned from Japan in 1952, speaking to enthusiastic audiences and showing off her kimono, her flamboyant public presence only made me more aware of my mom's reclusive public persona. My mom's timidity seemed to me a kind of lack, a kind of public formlessness, though she was quick to applaud and rejoice at her sister Lydia's bold public presence. Indeed, Lydia and my mom were dear to each other, and my mom did not seem to mind the discrepancy that developed during the 1950s in their individual social expressions and interactions.

2.

> *... I vividly recall playing Snakes and Ladders with Aunt Helen. She would always have a sympathetic sigh whenever I slid down a long snake, and when her luck sent her for a slide she always had a good-natured laugh. She never displayed a competitive edge. Instead she only wanted the best things to happen to her family and friends....* (From her nephew Phil Reimer's recent recollections of my mom during the early 1970s)

Whenever I asked my dad about my mom's reticence in public spaces, he would speak of her personal traumas in Russia and Canada, and of post-traumatic anxieties and lingering effects of those difficult experiences that tended to surface from time to time. But also, he insisted that during their earlier years of married life in Canada she had done her part, had played her role, had successfully performed with zest and zeal in the give-and-take of the social and cultural configurations that had been open to her. Indeed, during their first year of marriage (1935–36) she was involved in the United Church adult Sunday School classes in Stratford, Ontario, where my father attended Normal School; during the next eight years (1936–44), when they made do on a muskeg-dotted tract of land "up north" near Kapuskasing, she hosted countless Sunday guests in the tiny teacherage near his first school; in the winter of 1943, when he took on a neighbouring school, she—though without formal training beyond high-school studies in Winnipeg—with great aplomb took over his one-room school. And during those same years she conducted the school's senior girls' choir while he accompanied on the piano, performing in schools and in churches; she founded and led the Young Girls Club on Sunday afternoons; she helped organize the Ladies Fellowship Group at the Reesor United Mennonite church. Subsequently, too, she was active, during the five-year period (1945–50) when we lived on the campus of Eden, the Mennonite Brethren high school in Niagara-on-the-Lake, where my dad held the position of principal.

Indeed, I have my own recollections of my mom in that postwar world leading up to 1950. During that five-year period she still lived with enthusiasm, taking pleasure in her public persona. She socialized widely in the Mennonite community. She happily attended the school's cultural events, involving music or art or drama. Because we lived in a grand old house on the historic Locust Grove estate that in 1945 became the Eden campus, we ended up having to share the house with female students, for whom my mom was constantly on call; she helped them on various occasions, available especially to help or advise those girls who stayed in residence on weekends. And, of course, she looked after me, during what were for me my preschool days during the late 1940s.

But over the years I came to sense that my mom certainly "had been through a lot" (an expression used often in the Kitchener church about its members, including those who had once been extremely wealthy and then suffered greatly during the years of the violent Russian Revolution and its aftermath, and those who arrived after World War Two). In withdrawing from larger and more public spheres after 1950, she chose to experience them vicariously through her loved ones, as she remained actively engaged in conversations around both our table and my grandma's. But during the 1950s, she also drew deeply from her memory, unlocking the years that had come before: the magical era in Russia that preceded the violence, as well as some of the later (mid-1920s) years in Russia, and her first quarter century of Canadian experiences that she now treasured. But despite her withdrawal, the world of the 1950s, in Canada, in Ontario, where she lived, was a "good" world. Although it was not a space in which she could adequately create a plausible cultural identity for herself through telling her story, she saw it as "good" for me, and she entrusted me wholly to that world's institutions: the public school, the Mennonite church, organized and casual sports, the city's streets—all of these absorbed me fully, and she rejoiced in that.

3.

> ... In her extended family Aunt Helen was as an older, very loving sibling. She would sometimes act as a peacekeeper or mediator if I recall correctly (usually involving Uncle Hardy).... (From her niece Carol Goossen's recent recollections of my mom during the early 1970s)

But there was one other thing that my friends did not know about my mom, and this one was the most significant for me. Indirectly linked to her reclusiveness and to my conversations with her, during those baldly pragmatic 1950s she carried within herself remarkable unpragmatic truths regarding her life story, mysteriously beautiful memories that she did not quite know what to do with. The church of the 1950s, she would have felt, would have viewed with suspicion anyone giving expression to the kind of romantic enchantments of, and attachments to, the past that she so valued. Thus, in the social environment of the church, her personality was in an ongoing state of collapse after 1950. But occasionally with me she revealed reflections of those memories, during what I have come to realize were privileged moments. She could break off bits of narrative from her past and transform them into tiny glimpses of her earlier selves, selves that once had lived in the carefree brilliance and innocent hopefulness of her long-lost worlds.

Once in a while, perhaps on some Saturday afternoons or weekday evenings when both my mom and I were visiting at my grandma's, I sensed rather vaguely that those glimpses were but bare notations hinting at, or maybe even hiding, a vaster account. By a kind of accidental and, at most, occasional eavesdropping I came to realize that those fragmented intimations of her enigmatic world—a panorama filled with interlocking webs of people in high and low places in some incredibly fascinating corners of Russia and, during the late 1920s, in Winnipeg, and of fateful moments that swung between modest opulence and dire poverty—were an integral part of her normal discourse with her extended family. Indeed, while I did homework or read one of my books in the kitchen, my mother would converse animatedly of an exotic past in the living room. It was a past in which she, her mother, and her siblings had been players. In that friendly and relaxed environment where my unintentional eavesdropping was indiscernible to her, she endlessly retold a story—her story, of things now invisible—that she was chafing to tell others, but without anxiety or embarrassment. In that setting, I could tell that she and her family were speaking freely and happily with each other. It felt to me as though they were observing encyclopedic and primarily "Mennonite" details like those of a Proustian novel, with people, wealthy and less wealthy, well-known and less well-known, carrying out the ambitions of their profoundly optimistic motives and enacting events that involved grand gestures.

But sadly, with me she could only hint at that magic, for my ears—perhaps like the ears of many others at that time—were too dull, too inexperienced, too seduced by the attractions of the immediate present to be interested in what she had to offer. Nonetheless, now and then, she drew on her inner eye to train my heart, to affect my way of seeing. Her perhaps unselfconscious attempt to convey to me those brief yet vivid images of worlds far beyond the everyday world of our life in Canada in the 1950s, with its practical demands and religious orthodoxies, was one of her great gifts to me, as I finally see now. In small portions she made palpable for me delicate and subtle readings—ever clothed in her expansive expressions of gratitude—of the world's fragile and fleeting offerings of goodness and beauty, whether epic or minute in their dramatic scope. Her vivid recollections and projections made room for what eventually developed into some of my own presuppositions and affirmations: for example, my community-based interest in supporting energies and efforts that attempt to make space for the production and appreciation of visual and literary art at local and regional levels.

Here is an image that left me with a sense of wonder: that of my mother, without feeling any need to contextualize, offering up sweet evocations of Muslim calls to worship as she once heard them in Russia during her childhood, melodious and melancholy calls to prayer that expanded outward from the minaret of a mosque five times a day. Those sounds blended with her blissful memories of her parents and a few of their friends imagining and then, with financial support coming from sponsors in the south, bringing into actual existence their own vast and ambitious estate in the distant "north," in Ufa, just west of the Urals, on property belonging earlier to Russian nobility. She heard those calls to prayer, too, during her long and terrifying flight with her family by boat down the Volga River and by train through revolutionary Russia, calls that left her more fascinated than fearful. With her family's barely established estate having had to be abruptly abandoned as violence mounted at their gate, the goal suddenly was to find someone back home in the Mennonites' Molotschna Colony in "the south" who would give them shelter.

How she would have loved to have told me how these calls to prayer fit into a finely woven narrative of her life, how these and ten thousand other memories when set side by side could be made to fill in the finely observed texture of her dramatically lived days in Russia, her early days in Canada, all those days before the 1950s came along, had I only stood still long enough to listen. But—for all the contact we maintained in my years of growing up—she and I too often eluded each other, and I heard only the patter of fragments. She might have felt that, described in any sustained detail, her world would seem too incomprehensible to me, too incommensurate with my own, too complicated to explain.

4.

> ... Of all the siblings, Aunt Helen was most like my dad. She never said an unkind word.... / When I was visiting I would walk with her to Grandma's and we would take a short cut in behind Zehr's down the wooden steps through the grove of trees.... / When she and Uncle Henry moved to the condo I remember seeing her sporting a new hairstyle; ... she started wearing her hair in a pony tail which would swing back and forth as she walked. She looked so cute. I had been so used to seeing her with the traditional 'bun.' ... (From her niece Janet Payne's recent recollections of my mom during the early 1970s and the early 1990s)

My mother was born in 1908 in Russia's Ufa district, where since the 1890s Mennonite farmers and mill owners from the south had made quick cultural and material gains in education and commerce. After six years (1906–12) in the settlement of Jelanskaya, her parents began to establish themselves with two other families on the large Russian estate of Kusnezowo. It was already laden with cattle and horses—an echo of her mom's congenial experience of 1902–04 at the Steinbach estate. But after only five idyllic years (1912–17), their fortunes were swiftly overturned with the revolution. The Reimer family with its five girls fled, temporarily managing to keep one male servant and one maid, one horse and two cows. They first landed back at Jelanskaya, and then in 1921 they headed south amidst famine and cholera. It was a complicated five-week journey along the Volga and then via a reluctant train that at times they had to get out to push. Back in Ukraine, in the Molotschna colony, they lived on the yard of Mom's dad's brother until 1924, surviving with help from the "American Relief Kitchen." With her dad wanting to join the first post-Revolution Mennonite migrations to Canada in 1923–24, it was my mom, suffering from trachoma, who ruined their chances. However, after that things got better for a while, and my mom experienced some of her favourite years: from 1924 to 1926 she got to study in the Mädchenschule in Tiege-Orloff, the prominent settlement where her father had been selected as leading minister of the Mennonite Brethren church. And by then my mom also had two little brothers, Bill and Hardy.

In 1926, when my mom was eighteen, another opportunity to emigrate arose. Although it was accompanied by a huge sense of loss and temporarily complicated by setbacks, including a delay in my mom's dad receiving his passport, they managed to leave their Russian home. Years later my mother would describe in bits and pieces some of the details of the terrors of travel through Moscow and to the border, and then of the lush beauty of the English countryside between Southampton and Liverpool. And of the Canadian Pacific steamship carrying one of those magnificent Canadian names forever a part of my mom's lexicon—the *Montroyal*—on which she with all of her family made the Atlantic crossing to Saint John, New Brunswick.

With luggage marked accordingly they were destined for Kitchener, but (according to an unhappy family legend) in a train-station episode manifesting the kind of intrigue that was possible among Mennonite church leaders not keen on the liberal attitudes of my mom's dad, things changed. His intention to join his minister brother in Kitchener was slyly sabotaged. Instead, the family was forced to travel by train to Manitoba, arriving in Winnipeg on December 1, 1926. They spent their first three very cold nights in Arnaud, where my mom's dad's friend, a Mennonite Brethren minister, took them in. He was unable, however, to provide them with the farmland that the messenger in Saint John had promised was awaiting them. So, shortly before Christmas, they moved to Winnipeg, into a house on William Street. Winnipeg was for my mom a gift, a godsend. She found it a golden metropolis, a deliciously English city offering jobs at Eaton's and within the homes of the wealthy. This was work that gave her and many of her friends a renewed connection with material well-being and allowed them to absorb a pleasurable sense of the kind of elegance possible in Canada. And Winnipeg also provided a warm setting for choir practice and church gatherings among her many Mennonite friends, old and new. She went to high school there, taking courses in English, adding this new language to her fluent German and Russian.

But suddenly, another uprooting, further displacement, this time from what had become their dear Winnipeg home, when my mom was twenty-one. They moved to Leamington, Ontario, where her dad thought that opportunities in the Heinz factory and on small farms would provide employment for his children. There, working in the private home of a doctor, my mom helped to pay off the *Reiseschuld* from Russia. She lived with her family another six years (1929–35), until she married the tall, dark, and handsome Henry Bernard Tiessen. The well-known and revered Reverend H. H. Janzen was brought in from Kitchener to perform the wedding, at my mother's insistence. She and my dad then moved to the very English town of Stratford, after which my dad began a thirty-four-year teaching career with eight years "up north." The time spent there, together with the years at Niagara-on-the-Lake, eventually became a part of my mom's 1950s recollections of a magical past.

But even in Canada my mom and her family were not exempt from anguish-laden setbacks and tragedies that left them feeling helpless and abandoned, that left my mom bereft of a solid narrative that she could use as she negotiated her way in the Mennonite world after 1950. In 1929 in Winnipeg, my mom's beautiful younger sister, Gerda, suddenly experienced a mental breakdown that permanently disabled her; in 1931 my mother's father passed away unexpectedly, breaking an important family connection to a wide national and international Mennonite scene; in the decade that followed, the family succumbed to the poverty that overtook the nation, and my mom's brothers, Bill and Hardy, enlisted in the military, hoping to ease the financial burdens of their mother; and in her childbearing years, my mother suffered two miscarriages of which I learned only indirectly, from my wife, after I was married in 1969. My mom took events such as these as God's will and did not use them to complain about her lot in life. But I suspect that they complicated for her the ability to give an account of her identity, to tell her story, during the 1950s.

When she eventually arrived in Kitchener, she found herself in the town her family was kept from entering in 1926. The Mennonites she encountered there emphasized solid performances of various kinds of "worldly" achievement; they focused on a certain degree of material well-being, and she sensed that they were uncomfortable with displays of failure and loss and breakdown. My mother, by this time, had given up on these sorts of Mennonite claims to a perfect order. And so, during the 1950s, without intending to do so, the church in effect rendered her mute; it complicated for her the nostalgia that found an ambivalent home in her desire to make known a world that human beings around her had once envisioned and, indeed, constructed, in pre-revolutionary Russia, in the Mennonite life she found in Winnipeg during the late 1920s, and in the phases of her life in pre-1950 Ontario.

5.

I always remember Aunt Helen as a kind person with a warm smile. She would greet my siblings and me at her back door. We would be offered juice or perhaps Canada Dry. We always got a birthday card and letter with some money. If someone was sick or having a tough time she was full of empathy. The last time I saw her was in the hospital and she vividly and joyfully described being under a tree in Ukraine at—was it?—Uncle Jacob's farm. (From her nephew Bill Reimer's recent recollections of my mom during the early 1970s and the early 1990s)

My Aunt Clara once told me that she wanted to have been a novelist; she too, she said, had had dreams. Perhaps such thoughts by her sister suggest something about my mom. My mom's feelings and insights, like those of a novelist's, began to spill out in tiny portions when during my preschool years she wandered merrily with me on the old Eden property in Ontario. This particular piece of land had in the 1780s begun as an Upper Canada estate, replete with a grand house and pleasant gardens. On winter afternoons she pulled me in a small sleigh under what seemed like towering firs, the frozen ground barely touched by snow, the wind soughing in branches high above, surely as she had heard it in Ufa when she was my age. In spring she gave me rides in a small wagon among fields of daffodils, chatting lightheartedly to me, singing, laughing with girlish delight at my commenting on everything in sight. Mornings, orienting me toward the Anglo world barely visible across Lake Ontario where Toronto glowed mysteriously at night—she listened with me to Kindergarten-of-the-Air, CBC's radio program with songs and lessons for young Canadians. Indeed, some of the earliest lullabies my mom sang to me were in English.

Some years later, in grade four, I presented an oral composition about Algonquin Park, where our family spent summers during the 1950s. My teacher commended me for a particular line, a poetic description of sinewy roads running up and down between dark trees. That line came directly from my mom. Years later, after my undergraduate studies, my mom was among those who helped to move me from math and social sciences to literature and film—and, still later, to the publication of a series of art books with work by Mennonite photographers and painters. In 1966, when I shared with her the impact on me of Joyce's *A Portrait of the Artist as a Young Man*, her response indicated a close understanding of its narrator's quest, its Dublin, its Catholicism. So when in 1967 I said my fond farewells to my home church—amidst rejoicing in those quarters tired of my insatiable desire to analyze and debate—it was my mother's "romantic" influence that allowed me my freedom to leave but also to return, if I should so choose. Through her own detachment from the church after 1950, she modelled a way of creating distance from the church body, without severing ties with it altogether. And I did choose to return, just when I was entering graduate studies. With a little help from people who were then creating breaks with the past and setting new agendas for the future, I re-entered a new kind of Mennonite Brethren church that was taking shape in Edmonton. And, against the conventional grain, I began writing movie reviews for an iconoclastic North American Mennonite magazine for graduate students, *Arena*, founded by my Kitchener friend John Rempel, who (like Rudy Wiebe four years earlier) had found new energies in the Mennonite environment of Goshen, Indiana.

6.

Oma Tiessen was always present, waiting patiently to provide us generously with slowly cut and peeled McIntosh apples, carefully stirred frozen Old South orange juice, or precisely scooped helpings of marble ice cream (strawberry, chocolate, vanilla). / She was gentle, kind, modest. Oma expressed excessiveness selectively, primarily through her exquisite meatloaf, shared among the whole family. / She sat upright on her cushioned wooden chair, next to the door in the living/TV room. Oma would patiently watch with an adult Mennonite's eye the salacious and often violent television shows chosen by her cable-deprived grandchildren. / Time passed. The TV glowed. Opportunities were not televised. / Sometimes, despite her best efforts, Oma would fall asleep on her chair, head drooped forward. We'd have to wake her for ice cream. Opa was there too. / The home was filled with warmth, very comfortable, and imbued with modest Christian devotion. (From her grandson Matthew Tiessen's recent recollections of my mom, at whose house he and his brother Chris spent many Friday evenings during the 1980s)

My mom died in 1994 at the age of eighty-six. She was suffering with arthritis and diabetes during her latter years, but was cheerful to the end. As I say often to anyone who will listen, I think of her every day, and miss her enormously. She had a kindness that exceeded ordinary bounds, a concern for the happiness of others, as though life depended on her expression of optimism. "I would still plant an apple tree . . . " she would say, echoing Luther's sentiment. I lament that I did not learn more thoroughly the tender poetry of her heart during those years when she and I grew up together in our overlapping yet separate ways.

Note: For their views of my mom after I had moved away from home, from which I have drawn the words quoted above, my thanks to Phil Reimer, Carol Goossen, Janet Payne, Bill Reimer, and Matthew Tiessen. The slashes in the statements by Janet Payne and Matthew Tiessen represent paragraph breaks and line breaks, respectively, in the original texts.

The Rempels: Rita, John and Henry, and their mother, Katharina "Tinchen"

Rituals, Rhythms, and Memories of My Mother

John Rempel

I saw my mother walking toward me as I was coming home from school. From the end of our short street I could see the worry etched into her face. In an instant her troubled visage was carved onto mine. Wordlessly, we hurried up the steps of the shanty and into the kitchen. I took my seat at the end of the small white table where we ate, waiting. *"Der Arzt sagt* ... the doctor says I have a tumour as large as a grapefruit in my stomach. He says I might die."

I froze in my chair. My safe and carefree world had been shattered. In my six years of life I had never been without my mother, hovering, holding, and later allowing me to wander through the neighbourhood when she concluded it was safe to do so. Now this hallowed life was under siege. What lay ahead of me was literally unthinkable. The time between my mother uttering these fateful words and my father parking his 1949 dark green Chev panel truck and entering the kitchen is a blank. All I remember is Mom telling Dad what she had just told me, and then vaguely realizing that the back-wrenching burden could now be unloaded onto his shoulders instead of mine.

It turned out that the tumour was benign. Within two weeks Dad went to the hospital to pick Mom up. I was wandering around our neighbourhood when our green 1950 Pontiac Torpedo approached. It was them, both beaming! I ran home and we started life over again. But the fear that in the twinkling of an eye I might be without a mother remained lodged in the crevices of my mind.

Because of the chaos they had both experienced as children in Russia, my parents did everything they could to give us a world of order and safety. On the practical level this meant financial security. On a more profound level it meant faith, tradition, and family. But the personalities they each brought to this shared calling were so different that we children often wondered how Mother and Father had been attracted to each other. My father, the owner of an upholstery shop, was self-confident—sometimes to the point of insensitivity—curious, funny, and quietly devout. My mother, the homemaker, was sensitive, affectionate—to the point of clinginess—anxious, and demonstratively devout. She was a serious woman, without a natural sense of humour.

When they first met these differences did not stand in the way of a passionate mutual attraction. I remember stumbling upon a packet of letters wrapped with a ribbon. I peeked into one of them and saw that Mom addressed Dad as "*heiss Geliebter*," hotly beloved. The infatuation flowed the other way as well, I discovered, when I glanced into a letter from Dad to Mom. So it was a surprise to me as a teenager, when I was riding along with Dad in the truck to take a load of furniture to a nearby town, to hear him suddenly burst out, "I had to learn to love your mother all over again. We soon discovered how different we were and how hard that was. In fact, at one point when my boss asked me to take a weekly overnight trip to pick up furniture I said no because I realized I might be tempted by women on the road." I was both stunned and honoured by this confession. While it was shocking to hear, it was also moving to realize that he felt he could confide in me. This knowledge also helped me to interpret my mother's longing for more affection from my father.

Who was this serious, affectionate, anxious, and demonstratively devout woman? Katharina "Tinchen" Tobias Ewert was the sixth of nine children—five of whom reached adulthood—of Maria Funk and Tobias Ewert of Waldheim, Molotschna, South Russia. My mother described her childhood as "golden." Her joys were many: school, especially geography class, Sunday School, and caring for the family's animals. There were three cows, two horses for driving the adult buggy, two ponies—Kookla and Maschka—for the children's cart to use for their own outings, and her favourite, the newborn lambs that arrived every spring.

My mother's mother, Grandmother Maria, was a woman of fragile emotional and physical health. My mother would speak of her mother with empathy and sadness, as she remembered discovering her sitting silent for long periods of time on the cellar steps. Meanwhile, it was Grandfather Tobias who baked the bread and made the cheese, following in the steps of his father and grandfather before him. Grandfather was the children's source of stability. He took them by the hand and walked them to school on his way to work as half owner of the village "*Konsum*," the general store. Predictable daily and seasonal rhythms were treasured by my mother already in childhood. The most anticipated holiday after Christmas was grandfather's August birthday. It was celebrated under the apricot and cherry trees in the garden around long tables laden with *Zwieback*, *Rollchen*, *Perischke*, and *Platz*, well-cured ham, cheeses grandfather had made, and potato salad with a samovar of piping hot tea.

But suddenly, like a crack of lightning, the seasonal rhythms were no more. The Russian Revolution of 1917 turned my mother's golden world black. She remembered the day the anarchists, who preceded the Bolsheviks, stormed into their schoolroom, announcing that the oppressive old regime had been overthrown! To make their point the bandits seized the portraits of the czar and czarina, hanging at the front of the room, and stomped on them so hard that the shards of glass flew in every direction. By 1919 the anarchists had moved from exacting vengeance for mistreatment of peasants to indiscriminate plundering and murdering. The leader of the anarchists, Nestor Machno, was rumoured to be planning a raid on Waldheim. Terror struck. In an effort to ward off danger, the villagers quickly agreed to deputize a local Slav and a German to negotiate with Machno. My grandfather was the appointed

German. He and the Slav representative were told Machno would await them on a white horse at a grove of trees near the graveyard. The village prayed, the deputies made a deal: a certain number of horses and cattle would be given in exchange for the guaranteed protection of the village of Waldheim. As Machno's men drove their booty down the street, villagers stood wide-eyed, watching them. My mother remembered standing beside her father as Machno approached. He recognized her father, turned his horse toward them, and bowed. My mother recalled the brilliant blue sash and the grey fur cap he wore.

In 1920 South Russia's population was racked by typhus and was nearing starvation. Only the arrival of aid from the newly created Mennonite Central Committee from North America kept the people in the area around the Dneiper River alive. My mother was one of the schoolchildren who sang for Orie Miller, MCC's coordinator, when he arrived late one evening in Waldheim. They greeted him with the song, *"Die Last ist so schwer und so finster die Nacht"* ("The Burden How Heavy, the Night How Dark"). It's impossible for me to imagine what it might have meant for a twelve-year-old child to sing those words. My grandfather, among others, was given the task of distributing food. He willingly took rations to people who were bedridden with typhus. He himself contracted the disease and died in April of 1921. My mother was inconsolable—she had lost the only person who had kept her chaotic life safe.

My grandmother rallied her spirits for the sake of the children and oversaw the reordering of family life, including bartering what they produced for what they needed. This reordering of life happened in other ways, too, both physical and spiritual. I have a photograph (that in itself is an act of structuring reality) of the seventeen members of the youth choir in those destitute years. I see the sorrow and loss in most of their eyes. But they did meet. And they did sing. During this time a religious revival also took place in Waldheim, with the preaching of Johann Toews, a Mennonite Brethren preacher from the United States. My mother, as she put it, "found peace" through his ministry. In 1925, when she "could grasp the meaning of the new birth more deeply," Tinchen was baptized by Gerhard Unruh, one of the ministers of the Waldheim Mennonite Brethren Church.

Meanwhile, malnourishment had weakened Grandmother to the point where she contracted galloping consumption, a severe form of tuberculosis. Tasks among the children were again reordered, and my mother was made the primary caregiver of Grandmother for the two years that passed before she died. My mother recognized the intertwining of physical and spiritual need in Grandmother but found it emotionally and physically overwhelming. Grandmother was emaciated and bedridden but seemed unable to die. One day the deacon of the congregation paid a visit. He summoned the courage, in my mother's presence, to say to Grandmother, "*Ewatsche, Du muttst stoawe* ... Mrs. Ewert, you have to die." "I can't," she whispered, "I'm bound to my children as if with chains."

Grandmother finally died in 1926. Immediately after her death the siblings—Isaac with his new wife Lena, Mom, Hans, and Agnes—applied for exit visas. As she waited for word from the authorities, my mother took a position as a maid with a Suderman family in Beloyezerkow, a western Ukrainian town. She later recounted that she had always kept a suitcase packed for the day when the visas would arrive. On a late October day in 1928 a telegram arrived for her while she was ironing freshly laundered shirts. The visa had been granted! Instantly, she put down the iron, clutched her waiting suitcase with a few other bags, and set off for the train station. When she arrived back in Waldheim, her siblings were already weighing their options amidst rumours that the Soviet Union was closing its borders. How long should they wait for a decent offer on the parental property? Within three days they sold it for a pittance.

The haste in which they had to leave and the uncertainty of their journey meant that only small tokens of Russian home life could be taken along. My mother chose her grandmother's elegantly embroidered pillowcases, a few small figurines, her Bible with a photograph in it of a much-admired Pietist noblewoman—Sophie von Liewen—and a single fork from the everyday cutlery. As she and her siblings departed they tearfully sang a melancholy folk song, "*Drum ade, du mein lieb' Vaterland*" ("Now adieu to you, my beloved fatherland"). On the train from Moscow to the border they looked back until their native land faded from view. They passed through the famous Red Gate, marking the border between the

Soviet Union and Latvia, with boundless relief, and finally, after endless waiting, Canada arose on the horizon.

On their arrival in Winnipeg their former Waldheim neighbours, the Warkentins, awaited them. When they had slept their exhaustion away they were taken to St. Anne, south of Winnipeg, to their sister Mariechen and her husband, Isaac Goertzen, who had left Russia in 1925. They were too poor to keep Tinchen and Agnes, so after a few weeks these two returned to the city. Word was out that maids were needed by Winnipeg's rich families. The Tabea Home for young Mennonite Brethren women, under the much cherished leadership of Anna Thiessen, welcomed Tinchen and Agnes Ewert to their ranks. About two years into her work as a maid, my mother set her sights on becoming a nurse. Her doctor advised against it, however, telling her that her body had endured too much hardship and did not have the stamina required for the vocation of nursing. She was crestfallen, but my mother's respect for doctors, and for male authority in general, meant that this doctor's word was final. (This heeding of male authority was a part of her culture, and also intensified by my mother's relationship with her father, whose combination of self-confidence and self-sacrifice made him the measure of manhood for the rest of her life.)

Fortunately, there were other forms of fulfillment in her life. One of them was the strong bond she enjoyed with her siblings and their spouses. Another was the attention young men paid her. But the pleasure she talked about most in later years was her opportunity to sing in the choir at the South End Mennonite Brethren Church in Winnipeg. This choir not only sang in church but also went on outings, including picnics. It was made up of both men and women, and apparently all the women's eyes were focused on fellow choir member Ben Horch, renowned for his good looks and his musicianship.

After four years in Canada, my mother was lonely for relatives and friends who had settled in Kitchener-Waterloo, Ontario. On her first visit there she met Henry, my father. She was quickly drawn to him but he didn't meet her exacting standards. He smoked, he made light of things he shouldn't have, he was not openly devout and not baptized. Nonetheless, when Tinchen returned to Winnipeg letters went back and forth. They couldn't forget each other.

As time went on, Tinchen made another visit east. This time there were canoe rides in Victoria Park and meetings with relatives on both sides. By 1937 they were both ready to make the commitments that became the basis for their marriage. On July 18, my father was baptized by H. H. Janzen into the Kitchener Mennonite Brethren Church. And on July 25 of that year Mom and Dad were married.

Astonishingly, they took Tante Agnes, my mother's younger sister, along with them on their honeymoon to Niagara Falls. Taking a relative along on one's honeymoon struck me as something only people who think that babies come from Eaton's would do. That suspicion was laid to rest late in Mother's life. In a conversation in which she reflected on her and Father's marriage, she assured me that she and my father had made love on their honeymoon and had enjoyed it. Henry was born to them in 1938 and Rita in 1941. I came along three years later.

When I think back to my childhood one of the first things that comes to mind is the rhythm that attended it. While in matters of tradition and family loyalty my parents were of one mind, the arranging of the details of family ritual fell mostly to my mother. The daily rhythm began in the morning with a devotional reading from the *Abreisskalender,* a page-by-page tear-off calendar read (sometimes impatiently) by my father, followed by both parents alternating with either a memorized or extemporaneous prayer. In the evening our parents often recounted tales, of which we never tired, of growing up in the villages of South Russia. I'm astonished, as I think back, that they did not spare us the horrific details of the revolution. When it was time to go to bed, we children prayed the prayer Mother had taught us, *"Lieber Heiland"* ("Dear Saviour"), and then sang a German church or folk song. One that I remember well is *"Weil ich Jesu Schaeflein bin,"* ("I am Jesus's little lamb"). Indeed, my mother knew most of the hymnal by heart. Singing always cheered her up, she said, so she would sing for us and with us. The chorales and gospel songs that she sang rubbed off on me. When I was older I discovered classical choral music and was thrilled to realize that I knew many of the chorales in Bach's *St. Matthew's Passion*, and could sing along with the choir.

The distinctiveness of the weekly calendar began with a sequence of events starting Saturday at noon. This midday meal was usually made up of *Borscht*, a cabbage, beef, and tomato soup, and *Bulche*, a tall round white bread that complemented the soup. My mom made this simple but hearty meal, she explained, because it was easy to assemble and would leave her unhurried time to bake *Zwieback*, double sweet buns, for Sunday. With homemade jam these *Zwieback* were our Sunday morning breakfast fare, providing the nourishment we needed to trudge the five blocks to Sunday school and church. Dinner followed and then *Vaspa*, a late-afternoon cold meal, with the remaining *Zwieback*, cold meats, potato salad, cheese, and pastries. For both meals we often had company—usually familiar friends and relatives, but sometimes recent immigrants and friends from the General Conference church in town.

Then came the seasonal calendar, also cultivated by my mother. For the Advent season there was a wreath with four red candles. One candle per week, then two, three, and four, to guide us in our anticipation of Christmas. After the children's programme on Christmas Eve at church we were put to bed and told that if we wouldn't sleep Santa Claus wouldn't come. On Christmas morning we heard him rustling below, decorating the tree with balls and candles, placing unwrapped presents under the tree. Finally, we were allowed to run down the stairs in the dark and behold a spruce tree ablaze with white candles and colourful decorations. On New Year's Day, immediately after church Mother turned to making the noon meal of *Porzelche*, raisin fritters, sometimes accompanied by *Plumemoos*, dried fruit soup. It was Mother who gave the cues for these rhythms, but she and my father carried them out together.

Our family rituals benignly ordered our lives amidst the disorder that my mom's bouts of ill health brought to her and to us. One night as a seven- or eight-year-old I was awakened by the sound of forced breathing. I wondered what to do and eventually ventured downstairs. I was shocked to find Mom sitting upright in our chaise lounge gasping for breath. This pulmonary condition continued for several years. Then there were little tumours (all benign) and numerous stomach disorders. Doctors soon ranked with ministers for her as heroes of the universe. However, as long as her health allowed her the strength, Mom organized a choir that sang for hospital patients. She also sang in the church choir and was part of a church women's society. As Mother's ailments worsened, however, these involvements waned. Father was a dutiful husband—willing to listen to her laments, ready to pick up prescriptions, but seldom overtly empathetic, at least in public. Our domestic customs and the memories of Russia they evoked were our one bulwark against Mother's fragile health. The grounding for these outward forms was her unwavering faith in the goodness and provision of God.

I became self-conscious about the elements of our family's life of ritual when the language of church and home began to change from German to English. We had a clear pattern at home: between themselves and with their friends our parents spoke Low German, with us they spoke High German, and among ourselves as children we spoke English. But when guests came to visit and the menfolk were sitting by themselves after a meal "solving the world's problems," my brother Henry and I would practice our Low German as we conversed with them. When other Mennonite families were turning to English as their domestic language, it was Mother—with Father's strong support—who made clear to us that we were not ashamed to be Christian, Mennonite, *or* German. At the same time, when we had English-speaking guests my mother's sense of hospitality meant that not a word of German was spoken, even between my parents. Nor was the fact that we children spoke English among ourselves a concern. My parents' concern was that we remain fluent in German. The linguistic shift triggered a movement in our congregation to have some English spoken in the Sunday morning service. My mother turned to the telephone to canvass members to stand up for an all-German service; Father followed suit by making the same case at congregational meetings. The language debate was accompanied by a change of role for ministers, at least in our congregation. Until this time they had been charged to be the guardians of the status quo, for good and ill. Suddenly they were charged with the task of innovation for the sake of evangelism. Neither of my parents knew how to negotiate this shift.

Consequently, our family rhythm was both grounding and confining. As we grew up, each of us children responded differently to this attempt by my parents to hold onto as much as possible of the lost world of Russia. When we were young, my older brother, Henry, was my role model for doing everything "right." He was dutiful, gifted in drawing, and pious. He would caution me against using swear words at home that I had learned in the barn where I was a stable boy. But then, in his late teenage years, for reasons that remained baffling to my parents, he rejected everything the Mennonite Brethren church taught, as well as the way of life my parents had chosen. My sister, Rita, liked the rituals, but not the confinement from mainstream culture that our church and our parents stood for. She left quietly.

Although I rebelled less than my siblings did, I too bristled at what was happening. Some of the evangelistically minded people saw tradition as a colossal act of inhospitality to new Christians from other backgrounds. Without the diffuse sense of inclusion that tradition offered, the only basis of belonging became the Bible, accompanied by borrowed insistences of its infallibility. My mother was caught between the fronts of this cultural, theological war. On the one hand she wanted to witness to Christ and his sufficiency for our needs. (I distinctly remember hearing her, one day, ask the milkman if he had Christ in his heart.) On the other hand my mother (and father) could live with my own burning questions about the Bible because they sensed my loyalty to the sacred narrative—among other things, my strong pacifism, something that mattered more to them than a specific theory about the Bible.

This wider way of belonging, which still had a resonance in the congregation, lessened the significance of things that troubled me. While the manipulative manner of one of our ministers and the small-mindedness of people who worried more about people going to movies than about how they treated their employees bothered me, our parents had become more tolerant, and the youth sponsors and two of the ministers were beginning to listen to the concerns of the upcoming generation. But the disaffection of two of her children (and sometimes three) towards the piety and religious culture she had so intentionally cultivated weighed more heavily on our mother than on our father. This was partly because she felt she must have been a failure as a mother and a believer. This intensified a streak of melancholy she struggled with from time to time, a melancholy that sometimes frightened me. I was unable to sort out how much of this sadness or depression was due to Mom's personality, and how much of it was due to the congregation's expectations. For a while, she admired the sanctity of two strong-willed and ascetic (the monastic reference fits) older women in the congregation. They combined an unmistakable faith in Christ with a legalistic attitude toward pleasure, and insisted on a rigid recipe of how one was to witness for the Gospel. Mercifully, for our family, my mother sensed the rigidity of the women she had admired and stepped back from their ascetic tendencies.

The worst times in my relationship with my mother occurred when this fear of the world resulted in her becoming judgmental. Sometimes she was willing to negotiate, and sometimes she was not. She thought going to see movies was wrong. But we and our "English" friends wanted to see films, so the issue kept coming up. Father acknowledged that amidst the sinful intimations of sex and the outright violence of some films, there were a few good movies. As a thirteen-year-old, I borrowed his line. My mother didn't know what to do. "All right," the staunch pacifist declared, "You can occasionally go to good movies but never to movies that have violence." I agreed but then yielded to temptation a week later when a new *Lone Ranger* movie came to town.

Because I had been baptized and wanted to live like a Christian, Mom would sometimes ask me to kneel with her in prayer, particularly at the beginning of the school year. She would invoke God's protection for all three of us children with tears and sighs. She called on God to join her in holding onto the offspring she loved more than she loved herself.

The most painful memory I have of my mother's angst is of a wedding I officiated at. It took place out of town, and I left the reception early enough to pick Mom up at a friend's house in order to give her a ride home. Something I said triggered an outburst of fearful comments about what this world was coming to. People were dancing at a Mennonite wedding! And probably they had been drinking as well! Is there no limit to their "worldliness"? That was a word I had grown up with that always made me shiver. I protested and then gave up. I drove her home, turned around, and headed all the way back to the reception and danced the night away. It was the only way I could shake myself loose from the grip of my mother's fear.

How could someone who truly sought the kingdom of God be so far from Jesus's counsel "not to worry about your life"? This streak of anxiety hurt not only her relationship with her children but also her relationship with her husband. During my high school years I sensed that there were times when my parents struggled to be good to each other. I remember occasions when my father unceremoniously hustled himself out of the house to work in the morning. My mom would call after him, "Don't you even have a kiss for me?" Once he just kept moving, and I was left to care for my crestfallen mother, almost like a substitute husband.

There were other dramatic farewells. I remember a reunion in Kitchener of choir members from the South End Mennonite Brethren Church in Winnipeg. I accompanied my father at the end of the evening to pick up my mother. Old friends were saying goodbye in front of the hosts' house when we arrived. Mother and Anni Guenther, a woman who had been a companion of hers in young adulthood, were in the midst of an emotional farewell. Through her tears mother cried to Anni, "If we don't meet again here, then we'll meet above." I recall those very words when my mother took leave of her younger brother, Hans, years later. Did this melancholy streak, this fear of never again seeing someone she loved, go back to the life that was stolen from her when she fled the Soviet Union?

The frantic need for control was Mother's way of coping with the brutal losses of her growing-up years. Her refuge lay in ritual, a plain reading of the Bible, and the secure place of a wife in the home. She manned the ramparts when they were in danger. But she had another side to her. When she wasn't fearful she had a warm, outgoing personality, and was curious to meet people different from herself. I remember observing these traits with particular fondness when I was an undergraduate in Waterloo near our home in Kitchener. I would invite classmates to church on Sunday and ask Mom if we could come for dinner afterward. I don't remember her ever saying no. The food was always worthy of the occasion—roast chicken seasoned with aniseed, or roast beef with thick gravy, followed by apple pie or cheesecake with cherries. Occasionally, she would take me up on my suggestion of a bottle of wine to add to the occasion. The conversations were full of give-and-take between guests and hosts. This was the Tinchen I loved, the one who brought well-being to others and herself through the ritual of hospitality, who was free of the fear that everything that mattered to her would be taken from her again. As I grew older I became more generous with her because I realized that her tangle of self-confidence and fear was not only the result of childhood trauma, but was also the combination of characteristics that I shared with her.

And as she grew older, the fear—and its worst expression, judgmentalism—became more and more displaced by contentedness. As I was the last of the children to move out of the house, I realized how much more at ease she was once we had been launched into lives of our own. She made a pragmatic decision to fret less over us, headstrong as we were. She cultivated, instead, a growing sense of gratitude, a greater surrender to God and to life. And added to that, when my father had his first mild stroke in 1975, the traditional arrangement of my parents' roles was suddenly reversed. I vividly recall her urgent telephone call to me while I was at work: "The bank just called. Father fainted in the manager's office. They think it was a mild stroke. Now I have to do something. What should I do?" That had always been Dad's question, and throughout his life he knew how to answer it. Now it was Mom's turn. As time went on, she had more and more confident opinions, for example, about the timing of the next proposed trip to his sister near St. Catharines, seventy-five miles away. She asked more questions about Dad's move from partial to full retirement than she ever would have risked, at least during our table talk, when we were growing up.

At the same time, my father changed his ways and began helping Mother with household chores. I remember my pleasant shock when I dropped by their house one day and found my father washing the dishes. And how delighted I was to find both of them in the backyard, painting their white-patterned fence together. Indeed, my most treasured memory of my parents is the way they gently adjusted their roles in their final years together. Mother outlived her multitude of ailments and enjoyed better health in old age than she had had since childhood. And seemingly, my parents' original infatuation with each other had, in the end, borne the mature fruit of contented companionship.

My father died of a massive stroke on May 25, 1977. In the first few hours before he lost consciousness my mother was with him, alone. She told him, among other things, how much she loved him, and asked him to forgive her for all the times she had wronged him. Although he was losing his capacity to speak, my father clearly forgave her. That encounter carried Mom through the period of mourning. Only a few weeks later she announced to us children and our spouses that she didn't want to stay in the house she had shared with my father. My first thought was that it had been Dad's dream home: how could she move out? "I want my own place" she said, and went apartment hunting. We children couldn't believe our ears! She opened a new chapter of life in which the loss of her husband was balanced by renewed cultivations of long-time friendships with peers and their children. This involved lots of letter writing as well as hosting.

It was also a season in which Mother and I had rewarding, personal conversations as we ate together, or as we walked together. How do I continue to trust God in times of weakness, she would ask? How can I be a better mother-in-law? What should I do when the old ladies I visit with get into arguments? At first I was speechless at this reversal of roles. Such big questions that don't allow for simple answers were the kind I had addressed to her. Now she was the questioner. That kind of exchange launched us into a new stage of adult friendship. The religious question was foremost for both of us. While we both believed that the promise of heaven was profound and true, we also needed to know God's faithfulness in the midst of ordinary life, in which meaning was often elusive.

In the midst of all that was ambiguous, I was grateful for the unbroken circle of friends and relatives my mother had. To show my gratitude I would invite them over to my place. I was struck by the fact that Mom, and for the most part her friends, now treated me as a peer and wanted my opinion on the issues raised around the table. I remember one particularly warm-hearted supper, to which I had invited her boon companions Susa Riediger, Sarah and Julius Riediger, and Marie and Nick Reimer. I hadn't had time to bake *Zwieback*, so I bought croissants. When I served them, these staunchly old-fashioned people wondered what they were about to eat. One of them spoke up, "What are they?" I was stumped for a moment and then in a flash of insight announced, "They're French *Zwieback*." Everyone laughed at my attempted sleight of hand.

In 1983, after a couple of short-lived illnesses, my mother concluded that she couldn't live alone any more. We couldn't talk her out of it. She wanted to move to an "old people's home" while she was still able to adjust to a new setting and make friends. She picked

Tabor Manor, a Mennonite home in St. Catharines, Ontario. Rita, my sister, and her family lived near there, and since Rita had, with time, become like a peer to Mom and had also become Mom's primary caregiver, this move made sense. Indeed, their old disagreements were gone. And, almost unbelievably, our "sick mother" was now in fine health.

The years from seventy-five to ninety were a long Indian summer in which my mother helped out in the kitchen at Tabor Manor, navigated wheelchair-bound patients to their destinations, found her own way to church, and made new, and cultivated old, friendships. On one of my visits to her she excitedly announced, "I've found Mrs. Wiebe!" Who was Mrs. Wiebe, I asked? As a young woman she had been the nurse who had cared for our grandmother for months when she was bedridden at Bethania Hospital in the Molotschna. My mother's gratitude then and now was boundless. So we went to see Mrs. Wiebe, a still-elegant lady in her nineties. She simply smiled as my mother—and then I—thanked her for her care during a time of chaos and, for my mother, exhaustion. Then she said, "Your grandmother was very fragile but she was peaceful."

During these fifteen golden years of gentle aging my mother spoke of her struggles of faith with a candour I had never heard before. "How can we keep believing in God's goodness when our lives and our neighbours' lives have so much loss and sadness?" "Sometimes I think that the sins and weaknesses in my life are too great for God to forgive." Her soul-searching, without the quick answers of the past, drew me to her. During one telephone conversation she was brooding deeply and needed a comforting word. I was stumped. Finally I replied, "Mom, could you pray this prayer, *"Herr, ich glaube. Hilf meinem Unglauben."* (Lord, I believe, help my unbelief)? "That's a wonderful prayer, that I can pray," she replied.

After her ninetieth year the Indian summer began to wane. Winter was approaching. I remember another one of her prayers during the change of seasons, "Dear God, I'm no better than any of the others but please don't let me lose my mind." Relatives and friends continued to visit. My sister became her almost daily companion. Living far away, I cultivated our friendship by telephone. Despite her prayer, Mother was losing patches of her mind, but there were still lucid pieces of conversation, some memories, and often almost perfect recitations from the hymnal. Increasingly during the waning years of her life the language my mother and I spoke was the language of hymns. I learned to have the German hymnal in front of me in order to keep up with her.

During her last half year Mom barely spoke. Once the nurses feared the end had come, so I drove up to the old folks' home from Elkhart, Indiana, where I was teaching. Drawing on the wisdom of the friend who had accompanied me on this hard journey, I was able to consider my mother's silences as communication and presence, rather than as absence. One day after a long, long silence Mom looked at me and said in a strong, peaceful voice, "Now I'm completely surrendered to God." After that there was only silence again. It was then I thought of another language we had in common, that of ritual. I asked her if she would like to take Communion. She nodded. I asked two of her faithful friends in her infirmity to join us. The three of us entered Mother's silence with her. Then we went through the service. I made sure to include the confession of sin in case there were sins, or a fear of sin, to be confessed. And finally the words of institution, "*Der Herr Jesus, in der Nacht da er verraten war . . .*" (the Lord Jesus, in the night when he was betrayed). My mother's eyes were her words: focused, deep, receptive. She ate the bread and sipped the wine as if they were the food of eternal life.

She seemed to be ready but she didn't die then. Was she preparing? Was something still unresolved? Rita stayed with her for weeks and weeks in the silence. Five months later my mother finally died. I was comforted by the thought that at the Communion service she had taken unto herself everything she needed for the journey.

My mother was a survivor, but a wounded one. Both her woundedness and her psychological health arose out of her past. Many of her friends found well-being in leaving the past behind, but she insisted on binding herself in solidarity to her parents and their parents. My mother first taught me the meaning of the communion of saints. She sought the intensity of their faith and, paradoxically, knew that you can't hold onto faith without singing, without bread and wine, without being part of the bigger story. I am most fully in her debt for this grounding reality.

Lois and Josiah

Gifts from My Mother

Josiah Neufeld

The morning was grey and thin as cloth when my mother and I came down to the beach. The surface of the bay was flat, the colour of aluminum. We sat on a wet cedar log abandoned by the tide. I set the table on a water-worn stump: two teacups, a Thermos full of milky tea, two oat scones hot from the oven. We sat side by side on the log to share our breakfast picnic. As the low swells unfurled themselves like a lace-edged tablecloth against the gravel beach, we talked about the difficult thing we had been circling all summer: my straying faith.

My beliefs had been adrift from their conservative Mennonite moorings for some time. Sitting there with my mother on the beach, I could feel the tug of the various currents of thought that had drawn me out into new and liberating waters. But I could also understand my mother's fear. "The one who doubts is like a wave of the sea, driven and tossed by the wind," the apostle James warned.

I tried to reassure her. "Sometimes you have to go away before you can come back." I inscribed an arc against the sea with my arm. Believing, doubting, interrogating, redefining the boundaries of my beliefs—these are recurring patterns in my life. "I guess right now I'm outbound again," I said.

My mother listened, nodding, her elbows on her knees, her back rounded, cupping her teacup as though its warmth between her hands was a comfort. I'd been looking for an opportunity to talk with her about this, not because I wanted to persuade her of anything I believed or even remind her of what we still shared, but to ask her not to be afraid for me, not to worry. I know it isn't an easy request for a mother to grant a wandering son, especially a devout mother who has devoted her constant prayers and the best energies of her life to nurturing her children's faith. What I wanted to remind her of—though I didn't have the words to explain it just then—was that she, more than anyone, has shaped the person I am today. It was she who taught me to question dogma, to look for the face of God in all people, and to treat others with love and respect. She was the one who helped me carve the oars I now use to navigate foreign waters.

A memory of my mother: I am following her through a West African marketplace, through smells that simmer in the air under a patchwork of sun-heated tin roofs: ripening pyramids of tomatoes, pungent sun-dried fish that look like black, shrivelled croissants, fermenting bouillon balls, bean cakes sizzling in oil. Her sandals slap against her heels as she walks from one vegetable stand to another. She probes the flesh of mangoes, hefts a bristly yam, sniffs a papaya for ripeness. Two eager boys trail us, weighed down with bags and baskets of my mother's purchases. My legs ache. The sun is an oppressor. "Mom, can we go now?"

"Yes. Keep your eye open for a taxi."

But there's always one more thing. "*Mama Africa! Concombres. Bon prix! Bon prix!*" someone shouts. She stops to examine the cucumbers. She can never resist a bargain. The market women call her "Mama Africa." It's a compliment. My mother has learned this about West African culture: you dress up to go out. She wears a regal outfit tailored from genuine Dutch wax cloth—a wraparound skirt, a blouse with puffed sleeves, a headscarf tied with a peacock flourish. The headscarf is her crown, establishing her as a respected woman of means, a provider who takes good care of her family.

This picture of my mother, assembled from my memories, echoes an image from Greek myth: Demeter, the goddess of grain and fertility. Demeter is often depicted standing in a wheat field, full heads of grain brushing her sky-blue gown, a sheaf of wheat cradled against her generous bosom. Demeter, as an archetype, "represents maternal instinct fulfilled through pregnancy or through providing physical, psychological, or spiritual nourishment to others," writes Jungian psychiatrist Jean Shinoda Bolen.* Bolen uses archetypes from Greek mythology as therapeutic tools to help women understand themselves and their relationships with others. "A woman with a strong Demeter archetype longs to be a mother." She finds her deepest fulfillment in caring for her spouse and nurturing her children physically, socially, and spiritually.

Demeter describes my mother. Her own parents were Mennonite missionaries, sent by their church in Manitoba to live and work in Mexico. My grandfather travelled the state of Chihuahua by truck and horseback, preaching and recording Bible broadcasts while my grandmother raised six children at home. But my grandmother wasn't content simply to keep house and raise children. She hired a woman to help out around the house so she could teach quilting classes and lead women's Bible studies. During the rainy summer months she loaded her children into a truck and navigated mountainous roads to organize vacation Bible school in isolated villages.

Meanwhile my mother, the eldest of her siblings, pored over cookbooks and dress patterns, sewed her own clothing, and taught herself to cook meals that were nutritionally balanced and beautifully arranged. When my mother was in her teens, her family moved to El Paso, Texas, where she attended a public high school that offered a dizzying array of home economics electives. The school had two cooking labs with twelve complete kitchens and two rooms full of sewing machines. My mother signed up for classes in clothing

---

* Jean Shinoda Bolen, *Goddesses in Everywoman* (New York: HarperCollins, 1984), 171.

construction, food preparation, home nursing, family budgeting, childhood development, and interior decorating.

She doesn't remember a single boy taking any of those classes. It was the late 1960s then, less than ten years after a journalist named Betty Friedan had sparked the second wave of American feminism with her book *The Feminine Mystique*. In its opening chapter Friedan introduced "the problem that has no name." She described "a strange stirring, a sense of dissatisfaction, a yearning" experienced by a generation of middle-class American women who had been systematically taught that the answer to all their desires could be found in their husbands, their children, and a polished kitchen.*

My mother didn't read *The Feminine Mystique* and wasn't interested in feminism. Instead she read *The Hidden Art of Homemaking* by Edith Schaeffer and *Fascinating Womanhood* by Helen Andelin, a Mormon woman who offered advice on how to become "the ideal woman from a man's point of view" and improve your marriage by "prayerfully living your God-given role" as a wife and a mother.† Andelin's self-published manifesto ended up selling more than two million copies and inspiring a movement of women who saw feminism as a threat. My mother knew she had options. Her girlfriends talked about pursuing professions outside the home. For a while she considered going into occupational therapy or psychology. But nothing stirred her as deeply as the idea of being a mother and a wife. She met my father at Bible college in Canada and they agreed to orient their life plans around his skills: linguistics and Bible translation. He wanted to be a missionary; my mother wanted to be a missionary's wife.

In 1984, when I was three years old, my parents moved to a small village in Burkina Faso, a landlocked nation in the centre of Africa's bulge. They built a cinder-block house with a tin roof and my father began studying the language and preparing to translate the Bible. My mother experimented with the ingredients available in her new home—yams, okra, porcupine. She swept cobwebs from the walls and eradicated the tiny towers of termite dirt that sprouted overnight from cracks in the cement floors. She studied coffee-table

---

* Betty Friedan, *The Feminist Mystique* (New York: Norton, 1963), 1.
† Helen Andelin, *Fascinating Womanhood* (New York: Bantam Books), 15.

books of safari lodges and decorated her house with adobe couches, mosquito nets draped from bedposts, and Christmas wreaths fashioned from glossy mango leaves.

She also insisted on teaching her children at home despite strong pressure from her fellow missionaries to send us to boarding school. The missionary school was small enough that the presence or absence of her five children made a big difference. Every time a new school year rolled around, my mother negotiated with the mission board and fellow missionaries for the freedom to homeschool her kids. She finally agreed to send me to the school in grade six, but only because I was eager to go. The rest of my siblings did most of their schooling at home. My mother believed her children's first and primary teachers ought to be their parents. She stocked our bookshelves with historical novels and carefully selected home-schooling curricula that met her high standards. Together we learned how the ancient Egyptians embalmed their dead and how Eratosthenes calculated the circumference of the Earth using a sundial and a deep well 1,700 years before Columbus. We studied paintings by the grand masters of European art and read logic riddles aloud. "The round square furiously kicked the green yellowish." Could this statement be tested for fallacy?

Another memory: I am twelve years old. My eyes ache. My lips are chapped. The world is grey, painted over with sadness. My mind is treacherous to enter, like a room without a floor. I cry myself to sleep. I'm in grade six, at boarding school. I've never encountered such inexplicable grief. I think of it as homesickness, though the melancholy follows me home on weekends and holidays.

On March 8, 1993, I write in my journal: "In the morning I felt homesick. I felt hopeless. I wondered why am I living? What is my purpose in life? The feeling stayed like an ache in my stomach all day." A few days later, at home for the Easter holidays, I write this entry:

> In the evening I had a talk with Mom and she told me to write how I felt so I will. Almost all my life so far I have been a Christian but God has never seemed very real. I believed in him, but I felt like I didn't know him. Mom has always been like my God. Mom always had the answers to my questions

and took care of all my needs. I read stories about people talking to God and being comforted by his word. But it seems like God and I speak different languages. When I pray I feel like I am putting a letter into a bottle and corking it up and throwing it into the sea with faint hopes that someone will get it and write back. I never feel like I am talking to someone when I pray. When I read Bible verses, I don't really understand them. Whenever I have problems I bring them to Mom because I can talk to her. In a way she is the translator between me and God. If there is a situation where Mom doesn't have an answer and the only solution is to pray, I feel almost hopeless. I have never really realized this until today. Mom says that whoever seeks for God will find him, so I hope that someday I will find God.

During this period of existential angst my mother was my counsellor, my confidante, my spiritual guide. I remember talking for hours with her on the porch of our house watching silvery ropes of rain pummel the sand of our yard. She encouraged me to take my questions seriously. My mother believed evangelical Christianity was an intellectually robust world view that could stand up to hard questions. If reason was a tool given by God, properly used it would never discredit its creator. She gave me a book called *How To Be Your Own Selfish Pig* by Susan Schaeffer Macaulay, the daughter of Christian apologist Francis Schaeffer. I was hooked by Macaulay's matter-of-fact voice and her willingness to entertain precisely the questions that had ambushed my twelve-year-old faith. Macaulay assured her readers that the world pointed to a singular truth: "I believe that only one explanation of truth and life—and only one religion or philosophy—will fit all the facts. The other options don't work."

Rereading this book as an adult, I find Macaulay's arguments reductive and simplistic. She trivializes ancient writings and philosophies she hasn't studied, blaming Lao Tzu, Zen Buddhism, meditation, and drugs for our twentieth-century ennui. I no longer believe reality is a keyhole into which only one key fits. But as a twelve-year-old, I found the book's appeals to logic and reason reassuring. I was looking for a faith that could be scrutinized and a set of intellectual tools to help me do the scrutinizing. The tools my mother gave me are tools I have been using ever since to question and test the world view of my childhood.

Years later, living in Canada, I met a woman who referred to God as "she." I was astonished and intrigued. Mona had also grown up under the influence of conservative Christianity. The notion that God communicated mainly to men was something she struggled to liberate herself from as an adult. As she and I got to know each other, she taught me to see the ways in which our culture still privileges the voices and ambitions of men. When Mona and I decided to get married, I volunteered to take her last name. Mona said my decision made her feel loved, but my mother was upset. "I wish I could say that this is OK, but I can't," my mother wrote to me in an email. "I suppose you may think that there is such a thing as a family without a head, and that yours is going to be one. Or maybe that leadership should be determined by personality and perceived gifts. But I think that leadership in a family is God-ordained and that accepting and working toward what God has planned is the only way that both husband and wife's gifts will be best developed and used."

In her own wedding vows, my mother promised to submit to my father as to the Lord, "for the husband is the head of the wife as Christ is the head of the church." My mother has a strong personality and fierce, well-reasoned opinions that she doesn't hesitate to defend. My father, by contrast, is soft-spoken and reluctant to stir up conflict or impose his ideas on others. Given their personalities, I can see how my mother's convictions bring a certain balance to their relationship. When they disagree, my mother reminds herself to listen to my father and empowers him to take a stand. Though both my parents will say that my father's word is final, most of their decisions end up being collaborative.

But the feminist theories that my mother rejected have been transformational for me. Mona and I are committed to an egalitarian relationship. We make decisions together and try to balance childcare and household tasks in such a way that both of us have opportunities to pursue our passions and professions. After our son was born, I worked part-time from home as a freelance writer while Mona took parental leave from her teaching job. We took turns changing diapers, cooking meals, and spending long hours trying to soothe our son to sleep. When I was accepted into a Master's program in creative writing, we agreed that I would go to school for two years and then it would be Mona's turn to pursue her career while I looked after the home. When she went back to work and I became the full-time parent, I staked out my precious writing time in the early hours of the morning and during my son's naps.

My mother has always believed her calling is to influence the world for good by nurturing intelligent, compassionate, and spiritual children. And she has. She taught me to cook and clean and care for a household. She taught me to love, nurture, and teach children. She taught me to temper my own strong personality, to relinquish power, to think critically and draw new boundaries for the faith I've inherited. I look back on my childhood upbringing with gratitude. Yet my mother believes she has failed in her most important calling.

"What breaks my heart," she wrote to me recently, "is the realization that even though I can dedicate my life to teaching my children to think wisely and use their reason, to be kind and caring of others, to express their ideas vividly, to keep a home artistically, to be open-minded about different ways of thinking . . . . I cannot teach my children to love the Lord their God with all their heart, soul and mind. And that is the most important of all, and the Reason for all the rest."

Sitting on the beach with my mother as the restless waves troubled the pebbles at our feet, I was acutely conscious of the distance that had grown between our world views. I've come to read the Bible as mythology, as history, as a sacred text that has informed my heritage and shaped my culture, but not as a rule book or divine writ. In the figure of Jesus I see a feminist who struggled to subvert the oppressive power structures of his society. I think my mother would be happier to hear me say that I have a personal relationship with him. I don't think my mother has failed in her goal to teach her children to love God, but the words each of us use to describe that mysterious source of love and beauty sometimes seem irreconcilable.

Two months after our picnic on the beach I received an email from my mother. She had fond memories of our time together. "You very gently asked me to please not worry so much about you," she wrote. "I've thought and thought about that. I do have a lot of faith that God will complete the work He has begun in you. For me not to be concerned about what directions you are going and about your relationship with Him would be to not think of you as my son anymore."

"When you say '*mother*' or '*father*' you describe three different phenomena," observes Rebecca Solnit, writing about her own mother. She continues, "There is the giant who made you and loomed over your early years; there is whatever more human-scale version might have been possible to perceive later and maybe even befriend; and there is the internalized version of the parent with whom you struggle—to appease, to escape, to be yourself, to understand and be understood by—and they make up a chaotic and contradictory trinity."*

I wonder if the mother with whom I continue to argue about doctrine and belief is a version of my mother I've internalized, someone to push against as I assert my own identity. In that case, has she internalized her own version of me, someone to worry about? Perhaps me asking her not to worry is just as unrealistic as her asking me to return to my childhood faith. Perhaps it's a mother's business to worry, just as a child's business is to struggle.

---

* *The Faraway Nearby* (New York: Penguin, 2013), 34.

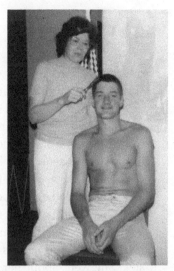

LaVerna and Nathan

Open Gates

Nathan Klippenstein

My mother is a fortress. Well, she was a fortress. You'd never know it now, watching her sit for hours on the worn sofa, surrounded by whatever my dad is able to find that might give her some gratification—a magazine, a newspaper, a set of old photographs, an alphabet chart. And of course the Bible and a copy of her favourite devotional, examples of the stone and mortar that she has used to build a solid barrier against the evils of this world, while diligently preparing herself (and us) for the next.

There is a large, well-preserved castle on the shores of the Caribbean in the small colonial city of Cartagena in Colombia. As I walk atop the four-metre-thick walls I try to imagine this hulking structure in all its glory, repelling the battering waves of the sea and the occasional attackers that threatened the city and its people within. It occurs to me that my mother was like this fortress: a stony wall impenetrable to the sins of materialism and self-indulgence, sheltering her children and anyone else who needed protection from the temptations of the world. She was a stone parapet of virtue standing guard over a moat designed to swallow and render helpless the temptations and stumbling blocks of pride, greed, and lust. At times I wanted to batter those walls with the anger and frustration of a young man who couldn't understand the importance of integrity and self-control. But then the roughly hewn timber and steel gates, like arms, would swing open, welcoming me and anyone else who needed charity, compassion, or forgiveness.

When I think about my childhood years I can see my mother bustling around the house. Throughout my childhood and even into adolescence I never saw her take a nap, or even once claim to be sick. She went about her daily domestic tasks and responsibilities with a song on her lips and a prayer in her heart. To her, housework and raising a family were both blessings and duties she took seriously. Indeed, they were to be enjoyed because they represented things to be thankful for—a roof over one's head, a healthy body, and myriad other things. Her vigour and zeal were to be marvelled at, and so was her creativity in keeping us children actively engaged in our chores. I would never have learned the multitude of uses for a small damp rag—removing fingerprints on door jambs and light switch plates, and smudges on religious music album covers—or that vine leaves needed to be dusted. I felt particularly proud when she complimented me on my carpet-grooming skills, or on the thoroughness of my job in scrubbing the sink and bathtub, using only the minimal amount of Old Dutch cleanser. My mother encouraged us to think of one Bible verse for every twenty dandelions we picked, and imagine that potato bugs were the dreaded plague that eventually led to freedom for the Israelites.

For my mother, cleanliness was certainly next to godliness, and complaining about work was not only sinful, but it also clearly showed that we didn't realize how fortunate we were to have all this furniture to dust, all this carpet to vacuum, and all these appliances to clean. Complaining that God didn't care how our house looked would bring a firm rebuke and a reminder that God was interested not only in how clean our tangible house was, but that He was also interested in the state of affairs of our inner selves. So perhaps praying for strength to do our work cheerfully, which I did, might indeed be a good idea. As I grew into a grumbling adolescent I didn't realize that the many lessons my mother was trying to teach us went far beyond vine leaves and potato bugs. Only once I got older did I appreciate that my mother's intent was to develop character by setting a high standard with regard to both our physical and spiritual surroundings. As we dusted and cleaned, we were learning the importance of obedience and stewardship.

Occasionally I would see my mother doing what she loved to do the most—writing. When the dinner dishes were cleared and washed, the laundry folded, and kids settled down before bed, I saw my mother seated at her desk in my baby brother's room, tap-tapping on Dad's typewriter, penning her thoughts with an open Bible or reference text beside her. As children we loved to read the most recent copy of the Christian magazine she contributed to regularly—to see if our names were there. She often wrote a column that was devoted to her insights and observations as a mother, wife, and follower of Christ. As a child I saw my mother as witty and wise, a scholar who only lacked the framed certificate on the walls. To me she was more than a cook, more than a housekeeper, more than a mother who applied a bandage when necessary.

In addition to domesticity and writing, my mother also reached out to others on a regular basis. As children we witnessed this almost daily: a package of food for an elderly neighbour, a sympathetic ear on the phone, words of encouragement to someone who needed them, cheerful exchanges with clerks and people she met in the street. Often she managed to quote just the right Bible verse or passage to remind someone or other of God's love. I remember on numerous occasions visits to "shut-ins" on Sundays after the church service—people who had few family members to visit and even fewer friends. It didn't matter if we were hungry, if the football game was already on TV, or if we were just anxious to start our afternoon after spending the whole morning in church. There would have to be one more small service, replete with Bible readings, songs, and sharing. We kids learned to put on a smile and cheerfully visit with those young or old who needed a friend. Or the two single men in church, socially and mentally challenged, who became regular guests at our dinner table. As a somewhat resentful adolescent, I didn't understand why these acts of duty had always to involve us. Why did we have to befriend and reach out to those in need? Couldn't we just be a little bit selfish and focus on ourselves for once? But no, a cheerful resolve and a purse that always seemed to produce just the right gift or token for a friend or stranger accompanied my mother wherever she went. And so, despite my youthful resistance, the seeds of compassion were planted, and a distinct sense of empathy eventually took root in all of us children.

I compare that zeal and resolve with the woman I sit beside now, and wonder how this could be the same person I knew in my teens, in my twenties, in my thirties. I wonder whether the effects of her stroke—the limitations of the brain—are able to diminish the strength of character within her soul. She was a woman who spoke eloquently to boards and committees, classrooms and congregations. She wrote page upon page, chapter upon chapter, sometimes for publication and sometimes for her own enjoyment of language and self-expression. Now she is reduced to simple sentences, and a few repeated phrases, smiling apologetically saying, "I can't say it, but I know what it is."

She waits patiently for a favourite TV program. This seems strange considering that when I was growing up the television represented a violation of all things good and edifying. Except, of course, for the annual Queen's address at Christmastime. Mom was sure to comment on Her Majesty's religious virtues, and how her message to the world reminded the listeners of the true meaning of Christmas. What isn't so strange is that Mom's current favourite TV program is a years-running gospel music hour. She hums the familiar refrains—songs she knew by heart and would have sung loudly in the church pew, switching easily from alto to soprano.

Indeed, one of the things our mother enjoyed most was singing around the piano during evening "devotions." This devotional time consisted of spiritual songs or hymns, Bible readings, and prayer. As a child, I enjoyed these family times, but as I grew older I began to resent these daily interruptions—outdoor games were summarily ended, the TV was snapped off, curfews were enforced, and even homework was put on hold. I became a somewhat sullen and rebellious teen, wondering why we had to be so religious. Church on Sunday mornings and often Sunday evenings, Bible readings before breakfast and every evening, mid-week youth meetings and activities all involving the church—was this really all necessary? I mean, how many saints did this world need?

As a child I enjoyed the Bible stories she read to us, and accepted as fact the miracles that were part of the Christian story. I also assumed the definition of salvation that our church taught. But as I grew older I began to formulate my own opinions and ideas about who God was, and about the significance, or not, of heaven and hell. From a sometimes insolent adolescent I became a rebellious and difficult teenager, openly resisting what my parents were trying to instill in me. But my mother was an intelligent woman, well armed with not just the word of the Lord, but with modern psychology as well. Her academic background in both theology and psychology was a formidable combination. She knew that the "wages of sin were death" and that "pride goeth before a fall," but she also knew that spiritual emptiness could be a deep, dark place, and that lack of a higher purpose could render life meaningless.

My mother's fortress had thick walls, unyielding to sin in its many confusing forms—greed, envy, lust, and pride. Personal adornments were shunned for second-hand clothes, and jewellery was frowned upon. A standing joke between my sister and me was that I got my ear pierced long before she was "allowed" to pierce hers. For me, it was a statement of social difference—a young man establishing an independent identity. I knew this would be considered a radically anti-social act that was sure to gain my mother's disapproval. Her look of disappointment when she first noticed the small silver hoop in my ear was all I needed to prompt me to remove the offensive item every time I returned home for a visit—even for years afterward. I wasn't sure if this behaviour of mine was hypocritical or something done out of respect. I would have preferred not to have felt it was necessary at all and that my acts of defiance could have been seen as simply that, defiance, and not some kind of violation of God's will for my life.

We were also taught to appreciate the things that we had, and if second-hand furniture and donated blue jeans weren't good enough, we were reminded of how little people in Africa had. We also had relatives in Africa who could personally verify that what we had here in Canada, we should appreciate. Looking back now, I can see how my mother was trying to teach us what were the more important things in life, that our physical appearance didn't matter nearly as much as did our motives for our behaviour.

We were constantly reminded to gird ourselves with spiritual weaponry lest the devil enter through a side door, disguised as something we might actually enjoy. At a young age I believed whatever my parents told me: "As ye sow, so shall ye also reap"; "many are called but few are chosen." But as a young teenager, I began to think: what if I didn't want to be chosen? What if I would rather be a sinner? When, for example, I challenged my mother's views of dancing—using the argument that it was a harmless expression of culture, of art—she was quick to reply, "If it appeals to you above the waist, it's okay. If it appeals to you below the waist, it isn't." Well, that response left me doomed. And what about alcohol? If it's so bad, why did Jesus turn water into wine? Don't bother trying to save me from going over a cliff; maybe I want to fall on my own. And maybe I didn't care what the Bible said, and maybe I didn't even care if I went to hell. And just maybe I just wanted my mother to say, "It's okay. It's normal to want to react this way. You're not a bad person."

Heaven and hell were very real places to my mother. She spoke about them with the same certainty as she spoke of a capital city or country we wanted to visit. As a child, heaven seemed to me like a wonderful place. We saw pictures of it in Sunday school, we sang of it in hymns, we prayed for it in our hearts. But what didn't seem fair to me was that even bad people could get to heaven, as long as they accepted Christ into their hearts. But what if they died in their sleep before doing that? They didn't have a chance. Eventually heaven and hell just didn't seem plausible. If the afterlife was only for our souls, how could there be physical weeping and gnashing of teeth? And what about the Muslims? Didn't they believe in their God as strongly as we believed in ours? And what if theirs was the right one? And if bad people went to heaven, could good people go to hell? Apparently not if they accepted Christ as their personal saviour. And so I did that, on numerous occasions. Being a good person was not good enough. Having faith was required for salvation, and if you didn't have enough, well, you better pray for more.

And pray we did. As a young boy, I recall being taken to the basement to pray, and asking God for forgiveness. This was not the pleasant bedtime, "Now I lay me down to sleep" kind of prayer, but the "wailing and gnashing of teeth" kind. Prayer was serious business; you bowed before God in humility. Guilt and shame became necessary companions, like dogs—watchdogs. How else to keep a sharp conscience to remind us of our failings and transgressions? And once again, if I didn't feel badly about sinning, well, I'd better pray for a sharper conscience.

My mother taught us to think of the devil as an actual being, whom we learned to fear more than the neighbourhood bully. Satan was eagerly waiting for us to let our guard down, when Temptation would creep in, unnoticed, and snatch another victim. We were reminded to gird ourselves, like the scriptures said, with armour to repel the constant barrages of evil's attacks. Daily confessions of sins committed, both knowingly and unknowingly, were required. I learned that a guilty conscience was a good thing and, fortunately for a young boy burdened by sin, that the relief of forgiveness and absolution was a short request away, absolved by confession, which I practiced regularly. And when I wasn't sure of God's forgiveness, I could always ask for the next best thing—my mom's. She became my confessor. I remember at the age of eight coming home from the park having just committed the gravest of sins. I had succumbed to the temptations of evil and taken a puff of a cigarette. Being acutely aware of how this act had left me far short of godly and family expectations, I returned home in tears and asked my mother's forgiveness, which of course she gave even before she knew what transgression I had committed.

As a young boy, the approval of my mother was particularly important to me; I felt acutely the guilt and shame of not living up to her expectations, for she represented all that was pure and good. She also vehemently rejected all that was evil and bad. The problem for me was the bad seemed to be a whole lot more interesting than the good. Later, in my rebellious teenage years, I argued constantly, trying to gain control and some form of autonomy from an authoritative and domineering parent. When none of her explanations about the inherent rightness or wrongness of some specific behaviour were sufficient for me, her final words, "Because it's sin" were spat out, almost like a vile poison, making clear to me that hell was a deserved place for sinners.

I compare the image of that woman to the one I see now, sitting at the table, trying—at times in vain—to follow a conversation, imploring my dad for details of events she can remember clearly but cannot communicate. Her eyes still twinkle when she laughs, and I am pleased that she can enjoy a personal story or incident that might even include slight irreverence, something I would have been severely admonished for in my teens. She always asks me about "the boys and the boys," her way of referring to the students in my grade nine classroom. Eventually her mind fades and I help her to the sofa. As I sit in a chair beside her, I sometimes catch her watching me with a kind of curiosity, as if wondering who I am or who I've become.

My mother's religious creativity was both remarkable and maddening. When I confessed I had been in a shoving match at a hockey practice, she insisted I take a chocolate bar to my new enemy the next day in school and apologize. A strapping at school resulted in me having to copy five chapters by hand from the Bible at home. I was sure the scribes and Benedictine monks of the Middle Ages gained more inspiration from this exercise than I did. When I needed to borrow some money for a Saturday night date, she insisted I put twice as much in the offering plate the next day.

I remember watching a British TV drama with my mother on a Sunday morning a while ago and thinking, "This is not at all the way Sunday mornings used to be." Sunday mornings were carefully orchestrated to have the family fed, properly attired, and in a fitting state of mind for worship, starting with morning scripture and devotional reading, and all before breakfast. Church attendance was never an option. Growing up I found it strange when I discovered that not everyone went to church, and equally strange that even my church friends sometimes were allowed to stay home on Sunday mornings. And when they were there, they were allowed to sit with their other friends, a privilege I had long ago forfeited after the minister came down from the pulpit to admonish me for laughing and talking during the service. Behaviour in public, particularly in church, was something my mother carefully observed, and a sharp look or a quick jabbing finger was all we needed to toe the line once again. She would often say that children's behaviour was a reflection of the parents, which only really made sense to me when I got older and wondered how parents could let their children act with such disregard for others.

It was understood in our family that discipline was my mom's domain. Not because my dad wasn't concerned but, as he would say years later, "Well, there are some things that matter more to your mother," and he left it at that. We learned at a young age that to ask Dad for permission would result in a deferral to my mom, and we would quickly reconsider whether the request was worth a second attempt. Usually she had a perfectly good reason for permission being granted or withheld, and as children we were taught that "talking back" was a sin somewhere between "Thou shalt not kill" and "Thou shalt not commit adultery." And so my mother's reasons were accepted with little complaint, at least not to her face. Thinking back to my teenage years I remember the frustration of trying to negotiate with my mom's stoic resolve. Not only did she always have a good reason as to why she allowed or disallowed our requests, but often there was also an accompanying Bible verse that supported her decision. I could be angry with her, but could I be angry with God? Would that in fact constitute the unpardonable sin? As a child I remember diligently praying that God would help me complain less, and then immediately following up that prayer with a request that everyone in the world would become Christians. I could count on a firm Amen coming from Mom's lips when those supplications were made.

My mother's formal education as a schoolteacher translated easily into parenthood. And a particularly astute teacher she was. From table manners to posture to enunciation and grammar, our mom had a sharp eye for details. Hair length, fingernail habits, and the way we walked were relentlessly scrutinized, and then corrected, if need be. We never questioned her authority. She was strict but fair, a quality not lost on four siblings each with their own personalities, needs, and behaviours. I cannot recall a single occasion when my mother even hinted that I—with great potential in academics and music, who resisted practicing of any kind and consistently settled for Bs in school—should be more like my older brother, who practiced diligently and consistently took home gold medals for academic achievement. Nor did she ask why I couldn't be more like my sister and younger brother who consciously stayed involved in church life when I stopped attending church as soon as I moved out of the house. It never occurred to me till later in life that the compliments and affirmations that I sometimes received from her, for even the smallest achievements, were maybe offered because she felt I needed them more than the others did.

We were always encouraged to do our best, but personal achievements, while something to be striven for, were secondary in importance to serving the Lord. A recitation in church received more attention than did a championship performance in Little League baseball, and hymns played on the trumpet always garnered a more favourable response than did a rendition of a jazzy school band number.

As young adults we were never pressured into any particular vocation or career path. For my mother, if we took seriously the admonition to "take up our cross and follow [Jesus]" whatever we decided on would be acceptable. And while I do recall her saying I would make a good preacher, I knew that she was happy about my choice to become a teacher. Certainly marriage and families of our own were occasionally hinted at, but never insisted upon. Travel and educational endeavours were fully endorsed, particularly when they included a trip to Africa to visit missionary relatives. The biblical call to be "in the world but not of the world" was instilled in us at an early age. A university graduation present of a trip to Cuba was given with the expectation that I accompany a group involved in Bible and Christian literature distribution. Interrupting my university studies to teach in a Mennonite colony in Belize was a fantastic idea. My mother could be a demanding coach, but she was also a most enthusiastic cheerleader.

As children we were taught to apologize with sincerity and accept blame without excuse, to love our enemies (or at least the unpopular kids in our class), and to "do unto others as we would have them do unto us." When the way of life of the apostles and saints seemed just a little out of my personal reach, and the expectations of Jesus Christ that were endorsed by my mother seemed too much to handle, my mother would remind us that God would never put a challenge in front of us that He felt we could not endure. And if Christ's example in the Bible was not enough for me, I could always look to my mother and expect her to demonstrate faith in action.

As I grew from a challenging adolescent into a rebellious teenager, I particularly resented the personal "training" that affected my social world, which for me was far more important than my salvation. I was allowed no community football participation because games were on Sundays, and I was required to come home for our family evening devotions even if I was in the middle of a neighbourhood game with friends, a curfew I thought more suited to an adolescent, not a teenager whose friends were driving and "of legal age." Childhood respect and obedience gave way to frustration and waywardness. Surely my mother didn't expect me to live with the same degree of religious zeal and spiritual fervour as she did. "Let your light so shine," she would remind us, one of many scriptural texts and admonitions she took seriously. To argue with her was essentially to argue against God's word. At times I could hardly tell the difference between her ideas and the words of scripture. Maybe there was no difference.

I resented the control my mother exerted over me, and her insistence that I live a pure, and what seemed to me to be rigid, life. I couldn't understand her concern when I arrived home late one night to find her sitting up, Bible open, praying and worrying about where her son was and who he was with. I only felt the guilt of once again not measuring up to her standards, and wondered why, if this Christian life was supposed to be so fulfilling, it did not appeal to me. Why did the dogmas and doctrines of this Mennonite faith/religion seem so difficult to accept? It seemed that for my mother belief in God and following Christ's teaching were not options; they were assumed requirements of life. But what if I didn't believe the way she did? What if I couldn't accept her way of interpreting the scriptures?

The imposing walls and battlements of the castle in Cartagena would take decades, maybe centuries, to depreciate. Over time the social and military fabric of the region slowly shifts so that a fortress like this eventually becomes a silent testament and monument to the far-gone past. But in my mother's case the walls toppled like the biblical city of Jericho—overnight, or rather one afternoon, while sitting in a salon chair. The stroke was swift and debilitating. And just as suddenly, I realized with clarity what my mother had meant to me. That night, by her hospital bed in the emergency ward, I tried to sing one of her favourite Low German hymns to her almost unmoving body and completely unresponsive mind. In that moment I realized that I was stronger than she was, and she needed me, rather than the other way around. My mother was, after all, mortal, helpless, vulnerable, and I had strength to give to her. All her religious fervour and zeal were gone. All my resentments and frustrations were stripped away. This was a tender moment when I was just her son and she was just my mother. The words to the song stopped and the tears flowed.

Over the months and years after her stroke it took all of us time to adjust to a mother who was no longer the matriarch and foundation that we had known our whole life. The writer could no longer feed herself, much less hold a pencil. This orator and compelling presenter and public speaker struggled to form single words, even the names of her children. The dignity of this modest and humble woman was laid bare by the necessity of putting herself into the caring hands of others. And yet, my mother maintained a stoic resolve to smile as best she could, and to greet cheerfully the many guests and medical staff who visited her throughout the long days of medical care. Occasionally when I entered her hospital room, I would catch her staring out the window with a sadness I had never seen before. In spite of her limited mental capacity she retained a profound sense of understanding. Occasionally I felt compelled to ask personal questions. I wanted to feel close to her, and I knew she appreciated that. Did she feel discouraged? Did she feel afraid? The distance I had put between us as a rebellious youth was gone, and I felt the contentment of a human bond, not between saint and sinner, but between mother and son.

Over the years I had come to harbour a great deal of resentment, and sometimes outright rebellion, against what I felt was a way of living and believing that didn't fit for me. As an adult it took me decades to come to a meaningful interpretation of Christianity, and a spiritual understanding of the religious ideals that I was brought up with. I needed to explore my own beliefs and convictions, not simply accept or reject those that had been foisted upon me as a child, as a teenager. I needed to separate my real self from the one I thought I should be. Abandoning a literal notion of heaven and hell became liberating. But along with that liberation came the sense that I was not only abandoning the religion of my youth, but that I was also abandoning my mother, who held so dearly to those views and who, I'm certain, felt the pain of mothering a prodigal son, a lost sheep. As an adult I deliberately avoided visiting my parents, and when I did I avoided sharing personal details of my life with my mother, knowing that aspects of my lifestyle would hurt her and cause her grief and pain. I wanted her to accept me, and so I felt I had to hide what I felt to be significant parts of my life from her.

Eventually I realized that I held more admiration and respect for my mother's strength and commitment than I bore resentment towards her strict religious expectations that were too difficult to live up to. Here was a woman who fed and clothed a family of six on a shoestring budget, often on what was then considered the poverty line. Later, as an adult, I would proudly reveal that as children we would gladly eat food that acquaintances on social assistance had rejected. My mother was a reuser and reducer long before the blue box was invented. Here was a woman who dedicated her life to her family while regularly contributing to magazines, journals, and devotional literature. She was a "woman's libber" who recognized that fair doesn't mean equal. The greatest gift for a woman was the ability to raise a family, to God's glory. I admired the fact that, like many women in the Mennonite culture, she made sacrifices—forgoing a career and pursuit of personal interests in order to be a faithful wife, mother, and, most importantly for her, a servant of God.

I grew to recognize the many gifts she had imparted to us, both knowingly and unknowingly. Often in front of my students I would provide an analogy or explanation after which I would think, "Wow. That's exactly what my mother would have said." I came to realize that much of my adeptness at working with groups of children reflected my mother's keen observations and insightful manner of conflict resolution. I developed the habit, like my mother, of clipping out articles or taking note of books that I thought a particular person would appreciate. As children we learned to be diplomatic communicators and sensitive listeners. We learned to formulate opinions, but never without considering the views of others. We learned to appreciate and understand multiculturalism and diversity long before these ideas became staples in modern educational curricula. My mother taught us to think critically and often posed a question starting with, "Now, why do you think..."

I also learned to appreciate the personality traits I shared with my mother—in particular a strong sense of nostalgia. Dishes in her kitchen were used daily for decades—yes, because they were still usable, but also because they held the memories of thousands of meals prepared with love and dedication. Worn pieces of furniture were kept not because of their style, but because on them the family had sat and visited for decades. For both of us sentimentality was a key ingredient in how and what we shared with others. Every object held a story. We were both orators and storytellers, and although my mother's hopes for me as a minister never panned out, I'm certain I have a good number of students who have felt "preached at" at some point or another.

My early memories of my mother, as for many adult children I suppose, are filled with anecdotes, recollections of incidents, and an array of disjointed events, some vague, some vivid, that are woven together to create my childhood, my formative years. To describe how I have become a product of my legalistic past is intentionally not to see the trees for the forest. For every unpleasant memory there are one hundred acts of love, care, and nurture, which may be less sensational, but which have nonetheless also had a lasting effect on me.

As I describe my relationship with my mother I remember singular incidents and experiences, and become aware of how the individual memories—many pleasant, some not so pleasant—have by now slowly blended to create a satisfying panorama. While specific painful events and incidents are still clearly etched in my mind, and while I can recall a teenage era filled with frustration, rebellion, and outright anger, I am relieved to discover that time and experience soften and smoothe, and that the resentments of my youth have been replaced with comprehension and appreciation. I have learned that walls are for support, security, and protection. My mother needed and provided those things for herself and for those around her. I eventually realized, too, that the heavy gates never swung shut on me.

The fortress fell in March of 2014. "Behold I stand at the door and knock"—funny how one of the many Bible verses we were encouraged to memorize as children comes to mind at a time like this. But now it wasn't Christ knocking at my mom's heart, and certainly death didn't bother knocking. While my mother's passing was expected, it was not entirely peaceful. However, it was not as emotionally traumatic as I was worried it might be. As a young boy, if I had asked my mother why people are sad at funerals, she might have said—with her typical insight—that we are sad for ourselves because we will miss the person who dies, but we needn't be sad for the one who has passed on because God promises us a spiritual body far more beautiful than the temporary one we have here on earth. I would like to believe that, but even with the saintly image of my mother ascending into heaven, I have difficulty understanding how heaven and a spiritual body are things we should look forward to. As much as I wanted to believe she would pass peacefully into God's hands, the frailty and fragility of life seemed so much more harsh and real.

There was certainly a time in my life when I knew I would not rest comfortably at my mother's funeral. I knew I needed to make my peace with her and ask for her forgiveness as a prodigal son. She had always taught and modelled the value of reflection and introspection. She had maintained throughout her life that grace came in the form of change and growth, and whether these were spiritual or human attributes they resulted in reconciliation and acceptance. I needed to tell her I was sorry for all the grief I had caused her. I needed to tell her how much I admired her strength and intelligence. I wanted her to know that I had often felt that I was created in her image, and that I was proud of the things I had inherited directly from her—an intuitive mind, a sensitive spirit, the ability to make a connection with whomever I met.

Despite the chasm that seemed to exist between us when I was growing up, I knew that my mother had been a hugely significant figure in my life. I remember in particular the occasion of my parents' fiftieth wedding anniversary, and how we children sang some of my parents' favourite hymns as family pictures were projected on the wall behind us. When photographs of a smiling, vibrant mother illuminated the screen behind us as the music drifted toward the congregation, I was choked with a profound sense of grief and loss. Seeing my debilitated mother sitting in her wheelchair trying to sing along, while we as a family did what she loved to hear us do the most, I realized what being her son meant to me. I really did love and admire her, and after decades of resistance I wanted to show her that love and admiration.

The day before she died, I asked my mother if she knew that I would be okay, if she believed that I was going to see her in heaven. She nodded and immediately folded her hands on her chest and closed her eyes, as if to say a prayer. The next day, she slipped into the heavenly place she had anticipated her whole life. I recalled a neighbour telling me that while visiting dying AIDS patients, he found that sometimes giving the person permission to die was all they needed to hear in order to release their desperate grip on life and transcend to the peace of the beyond. I wanted to think that maybe my mother felt that same sense of release. Although she may not have needed my permission, perhaps I needed to give myself permission to let her go, to let her know that I was sorry for all the arguments, the rebellion, and the resentment that I had harboured against her. I needed to forgive, not my mother for her lack of acceptance of me, but myself for my lack of acceptance of her. I needed to reconcile within myself the fact that I had not returned the unconditional love that she had extended to me her whole life. This was what I knew I needed to share with her, and wished I had long before she died. Behold, I didn't need to knock, because the gates were open. They always had been.

Byron and Evangeline

Fifteen Ways to a More Beautiful You

Byron Rempel

The appearance of the searching sun cannot warm hearts in this tundra. In the hospital, the family gathers on the cliffside of forever. We thought Mother would disappear in the next three days, but she sent death away and instead called for a hairdresser and makeup.

This is the story of Evangeline, who took her name seriously, the bringer of good news, who embraced evangelism like it was her namesake. You forgive me for thinking at one time that her church was named after her, the Evangeline Mennonite Brethren. One way to be Evangeline: all the way.

* * *

I was raised by a tribe of Amazons. The first thing you learn, before you bow an arrow, before you apply war paint, before you cut off your right breast, is that it is impossible to know all women. Women are not more tender than men; women do not talk constantly about each other; women are not wiser, nor guilt-ridden, nor man-eaters.

"You were indoctrinated," my sister Cari says on the phone, "into the world of women." In her kitchen she checks a to-do list beside a gourmet cooking magazine. Buy groceries. Get the Audi checked. Dominate the town council. What you saw was the best world of women, she says. We played together with hardly a fight until she reached puberty. The women swore me to secrecy: their reactions, their priorities, their loves. My sister apologizes; she has to go organize her world. Men may have appeared to be the leaders, she says. Dad came and went on his own secret schedule. "But the domestic dominated at our house."

"I know."

"You were a man in a woman's world."

My sister hangs up. She leaves for the town council meeting, her second term, the first woman politician in my hometown.

Once when my Mom's friend Jesus Christ walked the earth he broke tradition. He spoke with women and included them among his companions. Two hundred years later nearly all feminine imagery was erased from the one true church.

In the Gnostic gospels, the god of Israel claims responsibility for all creation. But that is only because "his mother, Wisdom, 'infused him with energy' and implanted into him her own ideas." He was a dupe; he wasn't even aware of his own mother. "It was because he was foolish and ignorant of his Mother that he said, 'I am God; there is none beside me.'"*

Nothing heretical there. Another teenage boy, built with hubris and bravado, constructing his own demise.

* * *

Evangeline's eyes are in deep space. I've crossed the continent south to north four times this winter. I have to know what she thinks before the great blackness strikes. Wisdom must descend then, or madness. Every moment of her life until then was guided by the god of her parents.

---

* Elaine Pagels, *The Gnostic Gospels* (New York: Random House, 1979), 57.

My mother's god was a jealous god. He was undeniably male, probably bearded, and thought Evangelical Mennonites were about as close to truth as humans would ever get. He was so jealous of other gods that he killed the god of her fathers, or at least critically wounded him. That god was more conservative and a lover of simplicity. But he was no match for prohibition, evangelicalism, revivalism; he had no immunity to cosmetics, polyester, and the internal combustion engine.

* * *

Evangeline's father navigates the treacherous ruts of Piney, Manitoba, and sings the "Good News" from the back of a Model A. His evangelical quartet is probably necessary, if only to push the car out of the mud.

Evangeline too sings through her mud storms. Songs can appear at any time. The dishrag in her hands directs an invisible quartet from the kitchen sink. She compiles a tuna casserole with different rhythms for each ingredient. Hits the highest notes in her duet with the floor polisher, especially when the frayed cord sends a jolt of inspiration to her heart. She invents her own soprano, breathy and with occasional notes beyond her knowledge. She's untrained other than in church choirs. She sang with her parents from the back of the jalopy, or followed Grandma's reedy whistles of tantric hymns to the eight-armed kitchen gods. While I grew up through my wincing teens, I spoke with care—each phrase or keyword could mean she would break out into a favourite song, a hymn, and, in the more difficult years, a dirge.

Even so, songs are chosen ones. Hymns. Religious music. Her influences she keeps close to her chest. I pull out three radical LPs from the home stereophonic system: *The Sound of Music*, *Oklahoma*, and the echoing strings of Mantovani. One Doris Day Christmas album, proclaiming that Toyland is joy land, "little girl and boyland." The rest of the albums serve up choirs, picked from a hundred-mile diet. No record exists of the moon-in-June groups of her youth, the Ink Spots, the Andrews Sisters. No Bing Crosby or Pat Boone, no Frank Sinatra or Elvis Presley, no Beatles, even in my older sister's meagre collection of 45s. Eventually Dad had an eight-track of Herb Alpert and his Tijuana Brass, but only because there were rumours of a family relation in management. When Dad jammed it into the car player, entire film scenarios spooled out to the soundtrack in my mind.

Mom stands at the door of my Quebec home, hates the finality of goodbyes. To my, and especially Geneviève's, surprise, she begins to sing instead. I forget the song. It's not important. Geneviève and I stand at the door, shifty, occasionally look in her eyes, look away. She sings louder. She is the diva of the Laurentians, and the deer and herons and raccoons stop in their tracks to listen. Evangeline reaches for hands and hearts and though her voice wavers and warps she never apologizes, no more than the wind in the pines.

Today Geneviève wrinkles her forehead when I fill up blank spaces with whistle and hum. "Did you whistle while I was talking to you?" I chase demons. The sound calms me. Or maybe I've inherited a twenty-four-hour soundtrack.

* * *

I am the son; there is none beside me. The only boy in a family of four children; the only boy cousin among eleven girl cousins on Mom's family fixated side. I am the favoured one, but only by default, not merit. I didn't see it that way, of course. I was sifted and prodded, molded and kneaded; I was ordained on my grandmother's knee to be a preacher, a bringer of the gospel. This is my *evangelium*: enjoy yourself. Time is later than you think.

I am neither a theologian, nor a scholar of religions, nor an anthropologist; the only thing I am versed in is vagabondage and word work. "We pushed you to go to Otterburne College," Mother confessed this year, "when you didn't know what to do." She looks into the faraway mirror. I shrug. The memory triggers a song:

> How ya gonna keep 'em down on the farm
> After they've seen Paree
> How ya gonna keep 'em away from Broadway
> Jazzin around and paintin' the town
> How ya gonna keep 'em away from harm, that's a mystery
> They'll never want to see a rake or plow

And who the deuce can parleyvous a cow?
How ya gonna keep 'em down on the farm
After they've seen Paree

"I know we pushed hard," she says. "Maybe too hard."

I wanted to make sense of what I was told, but I soon discovered that little of anything makes sense, or even tries to. The theology professors laughed at the grasping of philosophers who had tried before me—men like Sartre, Aristotle, Socrates. The theology professors took away my faith in faith.

Theology is the mathematics of god, and no wonder I failed, since I was never able to grasp the algebra of numbers. All I did take away from that time were two things, one of them helpful, the other a trifle. Juggling is a skill I still find useful to this day for entertaining children, small animals, and the easily impressed; but unicycles have proven to be a waste of time, and fit only for youth rather in love with itself. And who the deuce can parleyvous a cow?

* * *

Suddenly I need to listen to opera, before Mom goes to the hospital. Not the whole cow, but choice cuts. The great divas—Maria Callas, Dame Joan Sutherland. Mom doesn't say anything at first when she hears them. Only later she says, "I noticed that. Well. That's not like the performances at church. You don't have to worry that she won't make the notes." She is silent as they wail. I think she likes it, but maybe she's intimidated. Anyway, she says, it's nice to hear you're all grown up. Like when I announced I would now wear Man clothes, as I was fifty years old. No more sneakers and hoodies. "Finally," Evangeline said.

It was inevitable that I fell in with the divas. Bombastic, beset on all sides, tragic in love and not afraid to scream it. And that's not even mentioning the characters they sang. Beautiful too—La Callas like a sculpted icon of worship (*diva* means goddess in Italian). She strides on to the stage, and yes she is a pro but you are fearful anyway—she will hit all the notes but maybe she'll collapse in pain, or her tremolo will waver more than usual while she considers her thoughts, her desire will ever fly to thee, and her last breath of life shall be, *caro nome*, of thee . . . . Those flaws are perfect. Though she sings with the voice of a *casta diva*, a pure goddess, she is mortal.

My mother's voice was not always to be trusted. I grew to appreciate its imperfections. I don't sing in public since my high school operetta days, but I can only hope she felt the same way about my life.

"It has to hurt if you want to look beautiful." My grandmother said that.

* * *

The most important tenet of religions is appearance. The second most important tenet is to deny this. The way things look is much simpler to codify and follow than are amorphous beliefs like spirituality and truth. "For man looketh on the outward appearance . . . ."[*] This is our biological heritage, the way we have judged since the Stone Age; and it is not to be toyed with. In Quebec, where I sometimes live, the premier tried to do away with religious appearances and quickly lost her job.

If you are conservative, the importance is to dress modestly. This means clothing like everyone else in your clan, and with your references firmly and self-consciously anchored in a randomly chosen golden age (our former god thought the nineteenth century rocked). If you are more liberal, like Grandpa in his time, the importance is to not put importance on your dress. John R. was upset that people thought dressing plainer-than-thou reflected their holiness. His radical ideas got him in trouble with the church. You couldn't run a jewellery store in plain clothes, of course.

But this doesn't explain my family's attachment to the baroque. "Grandma always tried to look nice," Melanie says. When we talk on the phone she always does something else too: cooks, harvests wild plums, picks up after her all-male household. Her house is spotless. I can't see her but I bet she's well-dressed, with flair, even on the farm. "Maybe because Gram and Gramps were ostracized at one point. Maybe she wanted to show other people, 'We're of some worth.'" A woman should be beautiful, she taught her children. My

---

[*] 1 Samuel 16:7.

cousin Shirley says, "Gram was a powerful woman who was not easily crossed." My mother and her sisters are from raw pioneer stock; they all dressed and decorated their homes with elegance and extravagance.

Gram's brother was the town drunk. He came to her house smelling like ripe cheese and wayward milk, which is what she fed him. His more complex odours of neglected beer and spilled hygiene represented everything I thought our family abhorred; Grandma welcomed him without question.

My mother's father grimaced and stared, and when I knew him he had so few words left that his prayers over Grandma's homemade chicken noodle soup were sermons. "He was a thinker," Evangeline says in defense. He thought, as was fashionable at the time, that the Bible should be taken literally. Except where he didn't agree. Where women were admonished to "adorn themselves in modest apparel,"* for example. The adult Evangeline had suits of gold lamé, caressed and defended her furs, loved to watch the sun sparkle off her jewels. She commandeered the drapery department in her store with its endless swags and tassels and lace.

"Beauty is an aesthetic blessing," Evangeline says at middle age. She sits in front of the bathroom mirror, applies war paint, prepares to combat the plain and slovenly. Beside her, Father paints black his moustache and eyebrows. He beams at the comments from shopgirls—"you don't look a day over forty!" He has beaten death. He claims never to have had a childhood, and now disowns his golden years too. Raymond applies for the position as mythic god. There are no vacancies. He dies at seventy-five years old of an incurable disease, giggling at inappropriate moments from a wheelchair.

"I bless people by looking my best," Evangeline says. My sisters apply her makeup for her trip to the radiation clinic. "People may have a better day when they see you look well." Her cheeks and eyes hide wondrous tales of beauty in their wrinkles. When she kisses my cheek the aroma of foundation and powder rival the theatre. This blessing, she says, extends to all your parts. Get your varicose veins done! Fix your teeth! In the hospital she gives Cari some last advice: "Don't gain any more weight."

---

* 1 Timothy 2:9.

"What a legacy," Cari says. They stop at the mall on the way home from the clinic.

Stops at the mall are essential. Mother is on a quest to find the one shoe in the world that will fit her narrow feet. In Quebec she led a whirlwind frenzy through my village's shoe stores that literally left me dizzy for days. At seventy-five years old she could outrun me. She disappears in department stores as if she has Alzheimer's. But she knows very well what she's doing. I find her at the cosmetics counter, where the sales girls offer her a complete makeover so she's ready for the second half of her day.

As kids we knew we were different. We came from the fundamentalist backwoods, but we were rebels. Maybe not as extravagantly as on my father's side, who drank and went to war and gambled. But it was simple to rebel in my town. You fought with what you had; and our ammunition appeared to be dress.

Evangeline and her immaculate husband expressed themselves by dressing well, but we kids adored our "barf" clothes—our patched Saturday wear. As teens we fought to wear jeans, which were intended for farmers, my misinformed father insisted. He hated rips or tears or shoes not in their place. You can see where this is going. I embraced the punk era. I came home with orange hair, jeans in shreds, an earring, paisley slippers. "That was a bit of a shock," Evangeline confesses. "But I loved you anyway." Later, my all-black clothes were as disconcerting. They thought I looked like Johnny Cash, or worse: Johnny Holdeman.

* * *

"We dressed you so cute," Mom remembers. She holds a baby book, a meagre collection of black-and-white photos, a clip of hair, an outline of a boy's hand. I was her third child, and although the novelty of infants began to wear thin, Evangeline did get to dress a boy for a change. "You had twenty-eight outfits as a child. Dad reminded me to put them all on. Your little tweed brown jacket and hat. Your sailor's uniform and cap." In the picture, I like to think I have a rakish grin. The cap is tipped at a jaunty, seafaring angle. I must be on shore leave.

I was bundled off to Grandpa's barbershop at two years old, and hefted on to the cracked red leather chair. Beside its swiveling hulk dangled a great cowhide razor strop. My uncle, Grandpa's other barber, took great delight in assuring me he used it to spank boys who wouldn't sit still. The combs in Barbicide beakers like preserved skeletons. The hair clipper growled. The lamb to the slaughter.

"Most boys cried," Mom says. "You never did." Her thin white fingers reach out to me. She adjusts my hair.

By the time Grandpa closed the barbershop and jewellery store, Mom and Dad had opened the interior decoration store. My first job was to replace the scattered paint colour chips. I got distracted by the evocative names, escaped to the kingdoms they advertised, composed poetry with the discards, spent whole afternoons in a coloured haze. Who could resist Malibu Peach, or Devon Cream, Midday Blue, Pueblo Red, Café au lait, Mint Julep, or Persian Sand, even if they were all lead-based.

Eventually they set me on manlier jobs, mixing paint with a dash of Papaya and a hint of Saddleback. I watched as mother suggested window treatments to her clients. Big on the swags, heavy on the velvet.

* * *

It is only years later when I wonder what Mother went through, those years I travelled without contact. In her precious free time she imagined horrors. Now she says, "I pray that god will wrap his arms around you to protect you from the darkness of the world." Her god is a mother hen. Her god is a bouncer at the gates of pearl. The world looks dark from inside a closed community. And it does have its midnights of suffering, injustice, and cruelty. When you leave the gloom your eyes can't adjust right away to the sunny bits, the illumination. "All kinds of terrible things could have happened to you when you traipsed across Europe and the world," she says. Her fingers pierce the loose knit of her blanket. "You could have become a Buddhist . . . or worse."

"Thank god I avoided that." Buddhists attempt to lead a moral life, strive to be mindful and aware of their thoughts and actions, and try to develop wisdom and acceptance of diverse people, no matter their appearance.

* * *

My youngest sister, Madrece, is mentally handicapped. Well-intentioned educators and researchers tried to help Madrece assimilate. When new educators introduced their theories, Evangeline would smile and nod and let Madrece try the techniques. When they left, Mom shook her head and did things her way: she assimilated Madrece by paying attention to her appearance. "Easiest person in the world to help lose weight," she said. "You put the right food in front of her and she eats it. Done." Same thing with clothes and hairdos and religion. So Madrece had the patina of normal in the world according to Evangeline.

Mom sent me out with Madrece, no explanations or cautions necessary. No matter the phase—Madrece liked to grab at people, or pickpocket wallets, or toss random objects backwards over her head—Mom was sure I could handle it. If other people were embarrassed by this weird and wonderful girl, Mom laughed, that was none of our business.

Mom and I are on the couch. She is still, quieter than she has been all her life. Her eyes look through the mirror on the wall. Fine white hair molded, black-and-white striped shirt, a loose-knit, off-white blanket kept to her chest with pale hands. If she moves too quickly the room spins. She grins. "Madrece at one point had this obsession with feeling free. When she came home from school, she would immediately take off all her clothes and crawl between her two mattresses." Mom's voice is pharmaceutical. She squints through slender red glasses.

"Nakedness got extravagant reactions. She started to run around the house like that. She'd run down the street sometimes, you remember. One day one of your school friends came to see you. He was greeted at the front door by Madrece, stark naked and thrilled to see him. Got the shock of his life, poor boy! He was never allowed to come see you at your house again. . . ." Evangeline's eyes dance in delight.

* * *

We are a camera. Our eyes collect and focus light, then convert it into an electrical signal sent to the brain, which prints out the image. If you have faith in science, and accept Darwin into your heart, you'll know that our eyes evolved from organisms with crude light-sensing cells. Those organisms who could sense where light came from, or even detect shapes, nailed the two basic pursuits: food and security. Colour sense helped too. Sharp vision gave primates an advantage over our old friend, the snake, a recent study suggests. When they grabbed among trees, rooted among leaves, the venomous creature lay in camouflaged wait. That ain't no vine, Tarzan.

The snake was not always a symbol of evil in the garden, or sexual desire in Eden, a Judeo-Christian trickster. To the Gnostics it was a symbol for wisdom. Doctors use it as a symbol for healing. Resemblance to the umbilical cord also made it a symbol of birth and regeneration. With sharper vision, what snake do we see?

Often, *it* is not what it is.

* * *

I dreaded religious psychosis would descend near the end of Evangeline's life, that she would try one last putsch to rule her family's spiritual life. I waited with breath held for promises unkeepable, for arm-twists and emotional blackmail. Evangeline sat forward in the recliner and pulled the footrest in. She stared at me. "Your teeth are too small," she said.

I breathed out. Before, my teeth needed whitening. She'd worked as a dental assistant years ago, had since spread the gospel of maintenance and beautification. The nurses at the hospital exclaim, "Are those your real teeth? I've never see teeth like that on an eighty-year-old." When I wandered the hemisphere I hardly brushed my teeth, intent on proving her wrong. The attitude went with the ripped pants. That was followed by an expensive spate of dental correction. Now suddenly they were too small, and should be extracted and replaced.

This was indeed good news. Because I could laugh at her obsessions, not be offended at her attempts to standardize me. I dress less conspicuously now. It takes less than ever for a man to stand out: a hat slightly out of date, a European scarf, a shaved chin. But god help Evangeline if she tried to tell me my spirituality was too small, or attempted to change my secret relationship with the universe.

I look for a Hollywood moment at Evangeline's hospital bedside, a dénouement, a hand up to adjust an angel's tie. But there are only mumbles and tubes up the nose. Geneviève, my wife—my common-law wife, I'm supposed to say—came to Mom's hospital room. Mom whispered something, and Geneviève leaned over to hear the last instructions on the mystery of life. Mom grabbed her lapels. "If only I would have ... seen ... that jacket first, it would be mine."

Do not go underdressed into that good night.

* * *

Resentment at the bedside of a dying mother. What do I resent with the force of the father? Stuck there in a Mother Teresa dream surrounded by the ill and dying. Lotions and IVs, complainers and those with minds misplaced, frail dolls of senility who clutch plastic dolls; nurses resent visitors, visitors resent death, death resents the searching sunlight that streams onto the bed.

* * *

Another teenage boy, full of hubris and bravado. In high school I was sure I found *it*. I acted in musicals, sang to the gods, was thrilled by the attention from the audience, and the girls. One didn't have to be a jock—I could be responsible for artistic creation. Evangeline was even more tickled. Maybe it was what she had really wanted to do. Maybe it was pride in her brood. Whatever the motivation, her encouragement was limitless, and she sat through every night of the performance. I was so talented! I was so handsome! I was a juicy ham.

I got away with it at that level. But I knew it wouldn't fly if I wanted to be a professional actor. I acted on the surface, avoided the depths. To truly play someone, to give the appearance of reality, you had to perform open-heart surgery on yourself. I wasn't ready to go there—not onstage, not in front of all those people. Blood made me squeamish.

But I could do something else, something safer. True, you wouldn't get the girls like actors. But you could still invent, and appear to be one thing, and labour at another.

"You were my only child who cried because you couldn't read," Mom says. She can't read any more, not even her Bible. She can't focus. Her Bibles are memory. They stack on the shelves like idols. "You were four years old. And then you read everything in sight. Revelations, and the dictionary, and the Bible, and discussed it because you could remember. You weren't scared of Revelations. You knew it was a story, a fable. A metaphor."

Although she never believed for a minute it would support me financially,* when I began to write Evangeline believed I was the most talented author alive. Despite every indication to the contrary, I still think she was right.

* * *

The truth is a combination lock of... appearances. When I tried to get the codes for this story, my cousin Shirley said to me,

> As you are aware,
> the truth will be a combination of memories
> and individual experiences of
> and responses to
> the same events.

The beauty of that science can make me cry. Reason is so different from the didactic responses to truth I hear all the time. "Man looks on the outward appearance," the writer of 1 Samuel says, "but the Lord looks on the heart."

When I come to see her in what will be the last month of her life, Evangeline is adamant that I take her to the hairdresser's. Hair is life. She weekly maintained a style I called helmet-head for decades;

---

* Correct, thus far.

at my urging she finally let her hair go white, and it was dazzling. I was unable to convince her to let it grow and hang in a braid. It was time she listened, since she forever told my sisters to shorten this or colour that; their hairstyles transformed like leaves through each season. Every time I saw Mom I was told to comb my hair, from the first wisps at two years old to the last time we sat on the sofa. I never did. I like it unruly and incorrigible. It's important I appear that way.

My sisters get Mom ready for radiation treatment, again. They hover around her with coloured pencils and puffs at the mirror, pull earrings from boxes, fluff her hair to correct height. People are surprised when they learn how sick she is. You can't tell by looking at her. "She was the prettiest woman in radiation," Cari says.

By the time Mom goes into the hospital for the last time, she still has her hair done regularly. The day before she dies Heidi, her stylist, comes to the crowded hospital room, cuts her hair. They have to hold up Evangeline, drape her with sheets and a cape. They wash her hair, cut it short in the back because her head is always on the pillow. She can't even open her eyes. Melanie does her makeup a few times. She offers it another time. For her funeral.

"We didn't want it to look garish," Melanie says. "On a body it doesn't melt on. The makeup was difficult to do, but I wanted to. Heidi came to the funeral home too, she did her hair while I did the makeup. Mom had chosen what she would wear."

Melanie hates death. The finality terrifies her. She would rather mow the lawn than talk about her emotions with me, about what she felt in that cold room. But snow is on the ground and she has no excuses. "You can do amazing things if it's someone you love, that you couldn't do with a stranger. I don't know what they do in the funeral home with the eyes, maybe they put glue to close the eyes? But in one corner of her eye, there was always a tear, it always looked like she was crying. I'd wipe it away and it came back."

"Moving," I said.

"Moving, yeah ... I'm moving on outta here. But we tried to make her look nice. One of her last instructions was, 'And make sure my chin isn't so tilted up like on some bodies. I hate that.'"

* * *

Today I'm writing a novel whose main character is a woman. The work is difficult, but no more difficult than writing about a believable male character. Sometimes people say, "You love women. I can see that." It's true. But I've also hated women. I've cursed them, I've emotionally abused them, I've accused them of being gossips, of being wiser, of being guilt-ridden, man-eaters. I am guilty: I love their appearance. I love what they look like, what they wish they were, and what they pretend to be.

I never wanted to be like my father. My mother had the better deal. Father was angry, suppressed, resented work, resented losing his parents too early, resented he couldn't have been a professional athlete, resented so many brothers and sisters in his family. But Evangeline revelled in all that. She met with her mother and father and brother and sisters a few times every week while we grew up, and she laughed with them and fought with them and did what they said and defied their expectations. She took over the interior decoration store like it was her life's work; she took the horror of a mentally handicapped child and stubbornly turned it into a joy. And no matter what I tried to do or tried not to do, she welcomed me back and encouraged me and confirmed that I was indeed the most talented, most beautiful child on this earth. If I would just get those teeth fixed.

Elfriede and Lukas

Happiness in the Face of Austerity, Boredom, and Strict Morality: A Discussion between Mennonite Mothers and Their Sons about Dating

Lukas Thiessen

My mother was saying her goodbyes as guests departed my parents' house. It was evening, and I was about six years old. She stood near the front door at the bottom of a flight of stairs, while I stood at the top, looking down. Without warning her, I leapt off those steps and hurled myself down, latching onto her back in mid-flight. I may have caused her lasting physical pain as a result of this leap of faith, but she continued to care for me. She is wont to lament my lack of weight gain in the last decade, which I suppose is evidence that she believes I will not do to her as an adult what I did to her as a child. I share this story to let you know how much I trusted my mom when I was a little boy. This trust has not diminished over time. I still have the confidence to launch myself in her direction, although now I do so metaphorically, through conversations with her; I know she can carry my existential weight.

When I was a teen and young adult it was often difficult for people to converse with me, because I tended to push people's boundaries as part of my belief that it was good to make them uncomfortable; I demanded explanations. But despite my eager appetite for aggressive conversation, my mom had the patience to talk to me about all kinds of things. She even talked to me about dating. When I was in grade seven I asked her what I should do if I liked a girl. She thought back to her own youth, recalling her appreciation for a simple greeting from boys she liked. While it may not have been earth-shattering advice, it struck me as profound, because it never occurred to me simply to talk to a girl if I liked her. My mother did not tell me what I should do, but instead told me what had made her feel good. I think she wanted me to learn to help make myself and others happy. I have begun to see how much she cares about making other people, especially her children, happy.

Since my first date in grade nine, I have talked to my mom about the girls I dated. She would ask me, and still does, what I liked/like about the girl. If this girl made me happy, then my mom was happy for me, too. Sometimes our conversations went beyond just dating, and included the topic of sexuality. The most shocking of these occurred when I was in my mid-teens: my mom told me that sex is a universal driving force that affects everyone, including my grandmother. This revelation shook up my notion of who my grandparents were, and it also affected, hugely, my assumptions about the church, since I saw my maternal grandparents as something akin to high ambassadors of Mennonite church-based morality.

In fact, I realize now that while my mother's parents stood out as my archetypal Mennonites, as a teenager I also assumed that everyone in the church respected the same moral ideals, and would have had similar ethical responses to any given situation. But in fact, in recent conversations with my mom, I have discovered that the opposite is true: there is no conformity of thought and behaviour within the church walls.

Two months ago I asked several of my long-time church friends, along with their mothers, to be a part of a specific discussion about dating and sexuality. Through these informal sessions, I have learned that the church community's position on dating and sexuality has changed over time.

As I grew up, my parents attended a General Conference Mennonite Church in Winnipeg's inner city. Our family was particularly close with several other families in this church, the parents of whom had formed a close social group when they were in their dating and marrying years. These families still get together on a semi-regular basis. Even though we are not related, I consider the people in this group to be part of my extended family. During the course of the interviews I conducted with these same people, I learned that our mothers' dating experience while attending the church was very different from my friends' and mine. Our little group met twice in August of 2014. We met in Winnipeg's Exchange District, one of Canada's National Historic Sites, at MAW's Bar and Eatery. I remember eating there with my family as a six-year-old, when it was home to The Old Spaghetti Factory.

Despite my extensive studies in the academic discipline of history, especially Mennonite history, I knew very little of my parents' particular church history, and even less of how their romantic background fit into that history. What I had absorbed and understood thus far in my life was that to be Mennonite was to have your humanity denied in favour of an austere spirituality and lifestyle. I assumed that the people in my church learned to repress their carnal thoughts and feelings, and behave according to strict moral standards. Such regulation, lamentable to me, meant no rock music, no dancing, no drinking. But to my surprise, as the conversation continued with our mothers, my friends and I learned that our mothers' youthful experience in the church was not like that at all.

Indeed, it was the young adults of our mothers' generation who hosted wild house parties attended by young people from the church. Drinking, smoking, doing drugs, and, led by peer pressure and a gang mentality, breaking into a Hutterite community in the middle of the night whilst whooping and hollering, and then going back to do it all again—these activities were all part of the church youth group's experience when our moms were young. (These same young people returned to the colony later that night to apologize for their actions.) They even told us about an event at a youth leader's house where the youth leader's wife served alcohol to the young people gathered in their home. This shocked the three young men gathered at MAW's Bar and Eatery. We could not have imagined participating in events like this, events that were associated with the church. Other aspects of our mothers' collective church experience as young people—such as the location of the coffee house where they spent time, directly across the street from the church, and the fact that the "party house" was also nearby—emphasized the intertwining of their youthful, rebellious experimentation and their overall church experience.

This was fascinating to hear, because when we young men were the "youth" in that same church, it chose to ignore the fact that we were between childhood and adulthood, that we were often hormonally motivated, that we needed to blow off youthful steam. Instead of understanding this stage, the church chose to curtail youth's energy and curiosity. Certainly sexuality was not something we learned about through the church. I remember no sermons or Sunday school classes where the subject came up. Conversely, when our mothers were young, the topic of sex seems to have been approached from time to time. When I asked our mothers, "Can any of you remember anything coming from the pulpit that had to do with dating, or romance, or sexuality?," one of the moms immediately recalled her marriage preparation class, which had been led by a reverend who asked her and her fiancé if they had discussed how they would express their sexual attraction towards one another.

Our mothers also recalled the frank sermons this church leader gave. They also told us that he could be a very strict and morally demanding leader in the church. Whereas I grew up believing the strict morality of the church did not allow space for broaching the topic of sexuality, there was a time in the history of our church when a rigid moral code did not prevent the leadership from addressing this issue.

One of our moms told us that both when she was younger and also recently, people from other Mennonite churches saw our congregation as "the worldly church," a church with looser morals than other Mennonite churches. Indeed, all of our moms remembered the church rock band, the wild parties, and other questionable activities that were part of their church lives as young people. They also recalled how those activities were suddenly curtailed when a Christian revival came through southern Manitoba. According to our moms, this revival led to a paradigm shift at the church. Before the revival, our moms found the church to be a morally strict place where youth activities like partying hard were nonetheless possible. After, and as a result of, the revival, the church became a morally strict place, period.

Although the church itself became a place of restrictive boundaries, the congregation did not uniformly adopt this attitude. As we continued to talk with our mothers, it became apparent that the way they chose to respond to our dating experiences was with a quiet, respectful "watching over," without being particularly strict or demanding. One of our mothers explained her stance on this topic.

> Mom 1: *There['s] this whole idea that if you give too much instruction, too much guidance, that the person doesn't have a chance to experiment, or like, or be who they really want to be.... If you give them too much direction, they end up fitting into a mold that's not who they are, right? So that's partly [my husband's] point of view, and I really like that kind of thinking too. At the same time, I really feel like we don't speak it out much, like say, "This is what we would like," or that we didn't even talk about it together.... It was kind of left for "Find out how it's going," and like, a kind of trial and error thing, maybe?*

She went on to say that rather than enforcing a demanding regime on her offspring, she would pray, and matters would be sorted out.

> Mom 1: *And I'm thinking that prayer would cover it all. I would pray to God, and God would, like, He would weed out the bad ones and bring in the good ones [girlfriends], you know? That was also sincere. Like, praying was sincere.... I would pray about you dating someone, God would answer my prayers.*

While I was organizing the meetings between sons and mothers, some of the people I invited said they were not sure what they would say. Not because they had nothing to say, but because they were concerned either that they did not have enough experience with dating, or that if they shared their thoughts on religion as it related to dating, they might be perceived as pushing a religious outlook on those of us who were not interested in religion, since some of us boys are non-believers. But when the time came for our mothers to share their attitudes towards dating and the role faith played in it, it was evident that all three of them had chosen a gentle, caring approach.

Mom 2: *I would pray for somebody that is a believer, somebody that you would just really connect [with] on that level. So that's where my heart is at. But as far as talking to [my son] about it I never talked about dating, I never talked about ethics in dating. I never, I guess because we made a lot of mistakes ourselves, or not mistakes, but choices ourselves when we were younger. So, how could I preach something that I didn't live?*

Not only did they refrain from telling us what to do in terms of dating (for the most part, at least; years ago I had a crush that was not reciprocated, and my mom told me she was very happy I wasn't dating the girl), they also didn't pry into our personal lives. When one of the mother-son pairs was talking about the son's "on again, off again" childhood crush, the subject of a special love letter came up.

Mom 3: *How old were you when she brought that love note over? You guys were in high school then.*

Son 3: *No, that was in elementary school.*

Mom 3: *Are you sure?*

Son 3: *We were like grade four. Four or five. It was like . . . .*

Mom 3: *She actually brought a love note over but [he] wasn't home and so she gave it to me to give to him.*

Son 1: *Did you read it before you gave it to him?*

Mom 3: *No!*

Son 1: *Oh wow, that's respectful of you.*

Mom 3: *I never read it to this day. It was in his room; I could have gone in there anytime.*

Our moms told us they were concerned about the kind of people we dated, and spent some time talking to our dads about these and related concerns, but that mostly they turned their concerns into prayers.

Mom 1: *I found it really easy to pray about it, but I found it really difficult to put it into words, and to give you direction, and to give you, like or to kind of speak it out and say, "I want you to marry this girl," or, "Date these kind of women, these kind of girls." But in my heart, I was very worried. I was concerned about, concerned about who you would date, so I would pray about it. It was kind of like, like a safety thing. I could pray to God and God would direct you, because that's my belief. But I had a hard time speaking it.... Like, for Dad, it's a very private thing.... He would think, you should date whoever you want.*

Mom 2: *I see God as his dad first, and I'm going, "You know exactly who they need," and so I would just ask that He would make that connect. [My husband] was always the one who said, "Hey, what about this one for [our son]? Or, what about this one for [our son]?" And I was always like, "Let them make up their own mind."*

One of the sons said there was an unspoken expectation in his family that the children would marry Christians, although not necessarily Mennonites. But he knew that his mom's main concern was for him to be happy.

> Son 1: *I think back to junior high, we put on a musical, and I was Oliver Twist. And all of a sudden I had this like, group, I had these groupies, that were, like, calling me on the phone. These girls that I wasn't interested in. They would knock on the door, like, a couple times a night, even. And they would ask me to sing to them on the phone. But I was just like, Mom...*
>
> Mom 1: *He was the only guy...*
>
> Son 1: *I was the only guy in choir. I was the lead in the musical, right? And so this, like, and I'm, like, Mom, what do I do? 'cause I'm like, I'm not interested in these girls.*
>
> Mom 1: *What did I say? Did I say just be nice to them?*
>
> Son 1: *Just be nice to them...*
>
> Mom 1: *But you don't have to go with them.*
>
> Son 1: *But if you don't want to, don't do it... Your response has always been just about me being happy, and that's been really cool.*

I know that when I have shared my concerns about a stressful relationship with my mother, when I have asked her what she thought the right thing to do would be, her focus has always been on trying to help alleviate my stress rather than giving me specific instruction. She seems to be telling me that finding a way to be happy is the right thing to do. This response flies in the face of my assumptions about the teaching within the Mennonite Church: there I understood that happiness was nowhere nearly as important as were truth and righteousness. It felt to me as though something obscure and unknowable was more important than the happiness I wanted for myself. Realizing that, for my mom, happiness is a significant part of her faith, instead of a lucky break in the midst of a soul-crushing attempt to be a good person, is a gift that helps me on the way to a life of freedom that I have never found in the church.

I wonder what kind of relationship my friends from our congregation and I would have with the church today if we had had the permission to taste the freedom of a reckless youth, within the context of our church experience. As it stands today, not one of the three of us has very much interaction with the church of our childhood any more.

While youth group for my generation meant watching movies and discussing them, painting over graffiti, or playing floor hockey, our mothers tell a different story: *We were the worldly church. We had, we did, [pause]. We were bad.* What was most shocking to me was not that our moms were drinking, smoking, partying, or having sexual experiences before marriage, but that these activities occurred within the context of the church—not necessarily at church-sanctioned events, but with the members of the church's youth group.

Son 2: *We were not bad like you.*

Son 1: *Like, definitely not.*

Mom 2: *We were very bad. We were just terrible.*

Son 1: *We never would have gone drinking together.*

Son 2: *Oh no.*

Mom 2: *We partied there, it was just a block away from the church. It was terrible, just terrible. And our parents all thought it was wonderful because it was part of church group activities.*

Son 2: *We were not like that at all. We had a very different experience from you guys.*

Even the mom in our group who described herself as "not one to be wild" still spent a lot of time with the group that partied, and when she and her husband were first married they hosted parties almost every weekend, parties that included dancing and drinking. So if there once was a place in the same church for those who partied hard and those who did not, maybe there can be a place in the church today for those of dichotomous preferences, beliefs, and actions. Maybe the Mennonite Church needs to be a place where young people can rebel in extreme ways if they are to fall in love with the church community. Imagine a church that explains what it considers to be proper ethical behaviour and calls for a certain code of morality, while simultaneously proclaiming that no matter how you think or act, it is a safe place in which to be that person.

If the church could recognize and address the boiling yearning in the blood of young people, and see it not as something to be controlled but as something to experience within the context of the church, perhaps more young people would believe that their desires are not anti- or extra-ecclesiastical, but part of a worshipful life. Not that young people need encouragement or permission to push boundaries, or that the church should exude a lax response to behaviour that is harmful, but rather, that the church could learn, or perhaps relearn, how to develop social relationships that are open and bountiful while at the same time encouraging the moral behaviour it believes in. Maybe there should be a place in the church for people whose beliefs and actions are far outside the norm. Perhaps the church can address the different kinds of people in the world with a view similar to our mothers, a view that seeks happiness for each individual.

When I was in Walla Walla, Washington, in 2006, I visited my mom's great-aunt and great-uncle. I held assumptions about elderly churchgoing people in my family, assumptions that were immediately challenged by my ninety-three-year-old great-great-aunt who asked me, "What does your church believe about homosexuality? Ours is the only open and affirming one out here." It was exciting for me to meet elderly Mennonites who are proud to belong to a church that affirms, and even tenderly embraces, those who are openly gay.

In the two decades and more since I jumped on my mom's back and pinched her sciatic nerve, I have launched various bombshells in her direction. I told her I was moving out—only two days before I actually did so. I told her I was hitchhiking to Tierra del Fuego (I never made it there)—three days before I left. I told her about working at a sex shop, about various kinds of recreational drugs I have enjoyed. I told her I was an atheist and ran a social group for atheist students. I told her I decided to start a relationship with a girl who was eight months pregnant from a previous relationship and help raise her son.

My mom has always supported me. She and my dad gave me furniture and did laundry for me when I moved out. She and my dad gave me hundreds of dollars before I went hitchhiking, and more while I was stuck trying to get into the United States. She and my dad visited me at the sex shop. She joked with me that maybe she should try some of the drugs herself. (She never will.) Both my parents seemed nonplussed when I told them I was a non-believer, affirming, "Yeah, we thought so." Most recently, she found my old baby clothes and gave them to me so I could put them on my beautiful new son.

Lately she's been inviting me to come to church on Sunday mornings with her. One of the new pastors has also been encouraging me to get involved in the church, with the full understanding that I'm an atheist. Maybe, somewhere in the heart of the church, is the kind of mother I have. The one who loves you even when you're an aggravating, drugged-up sex fiend vagabond atheist raising a son born out of wedlock.

Maybe the world doesn't need God so much as everyone needs my mom.

Christoff's mother, Sharon

heritage

Christoff Engbrecht

i'm moments from going out
my mother sitting there
in her slip at the kitchen table

queen of rotundas
lazysusans, vestibules and chandeliers
of gorse and hassocks
and slow turf fires
insisting
she sew my jeans before i leave

"you know
my mother never celebrated st. patrick's day"
she says looking over her shoulder
to the calender
bee's wax wasp's nests and wet lake clay
she turns and smiles
handing me the needle

sitting across from her in my longjohns
i take the spool
between thumb and fore finger
unravel the timid blue thread
wet the end within lips and close in
to the needle's jackpine eye
follow the two lines to a length
as she reads to me a poem
she had just written

a poem about what had burdened
jesus' mother mary and helen of troy
perpendicularities of apotheosis and the vagina
the suffering from right angles of divine imposition
as i bite the thread
and knot the ends to one

she pours us each a glass
the only irish she knows on her tongue
"to tiocfaidh ar la" raising her glass
"to chucky" i reply
clinking our glasses
to this late night sew and whiskey moment

taking the needle and blue thread
she asks
what i thought of her poem

"are you sure that's how you pronounce vagina"
unable to keep from laughing
"and like hell you'd know"
she exclaims
waving me off bulrush

"can't you just throw these goddamned jeans away"
pointing out another irreparable riphole
and poking her finger hummingbird through

and we turn quiet
as though watching from the step
of the house on rice lake
the far off blinkings of fireflies
mapping cactus rock across the bay
the summer midnight's northern sky
in variform with a lone loon's cry

how many
gestures have passed this way between us
as she pulls the needle with a last tug
biting down on the blue thread

"here" she says handing me the jeans

"we'll sew the rest up next st. patrick's
now get outta here"
putting her hand to my face
"and have a good time tonight"

we stand our drinks down
and i leave out the backdoor

that i should have said

"but i already have mom"

queen of rotundas
lazysusans, vestibules and chandeliers
gorse and hassocks
and slow turf fires

Howard and Mary

Mary Dyck's Vicarious Life

Howard Dyck

> Thou art thy mother's glass, and she in thee
> Calls back the lovely April of her prime
> —William Shakespeare, Sonnet 3

First, a disclaimer. I have written about many things over many years: this has been by far the hardest topic for me. When one is as close to the subject of one's investigation as a son is to his mother, any chance of objectivity or even perspective vanishes in a cloud of nostalgia and selective recall, not to mention grief over lost opportunities. My mother was a good woman, not a perfect one; she was resilient, not heroic; consistent rather than adventurous. Hers was an ordinary life, yet she valued extraordinary achievements, especially those of her sons. She had little sense of history, but she filled her place in her time with courage, fortitude, and affection. In her own simple, loving, unaffected way, she shaped my life as only a mother can. To analyze such a relationship is to venture into treacherous shoals. And so I offer here a series of snapshots, vignettes, which, I can only hope, will do her justice and shed some light on a life well lived, a simple, honest, integral life.

Mary Dyck (born Mary Ann Wiebe) was born March 1, 1919, and died September 8, 2008, at the age of eighty-nine. Her parents had come to Canada from Ukraine in the late nineteenth century, met and married in Kansas, and settled on a farm near Winkler, Manitoba. My mother lived almost her entire life within eight kilometres of the family farmhouse where she was born. On the eighth of June, 1940, at the age of twenty-one, she married John Peter Dyck. I was the eldest of three sons and I first saw the light of day on November 17, 1942. I was born in the same farmhouse in the Zion School District in which my mother was born and raised. Evidently I was reluctant to make my appearance, emerging only after a long and bitterly painful labour, a fact of which my mother reminded me not infrequently, particularly when she and I had our moments of disagreement.

"*Fritzi, lauf, lauf, lauf schnell!*" ("Fritzi" was my nickname during my earliest years, then it was "Howie," and about the time I started high school I was promoted to my given name, "Howard.") My mother screaming in terror is my first vivid recollection of her. I was two, and we were living on a farm near Dominion City, Manitoba. I was playing in a pasture not far from our little farmhouse, and I must have wandered between a cow and her calf. The cow took off after me and would surely have mauled me had I not run for my life, encouraged by Mom's frantic cries. I scampered through the open door of the house with the cow hard on my heels. Shaken but unhurt, I recall being cradled in my weeping mother's arms. Not long after that incident we moved to the farm in the Burwalde School District near Winkler, where my father and his three siblings had been raised by his mother and stepfather, Abram Banman. That would be my home until I finished high school and left to pursue undergraduate studies in Winnipeg.

Ours was a traditional, content, and generally happy Russian Mennonite home. We spoke High German, although Mom and Dad spoke Low German to each other. Dad was the boss, albeit a beneficent one. Mom was subservient (*untertan* was the German word), a role she accepted and indeed endorsed, but which she came to view with a certain grudging resentment as the years passed and she observed the feminist movement in general as well as the quiet yet firm independence of her first daughter-in-law. Both Mom and Dad worked hard on their little half-section of land, wresting a modest but relatively comfortable living from it, year in, year out. By no means were we wealthy, but I don't recall ever thinking we were poor.

If Mom's obvious role was cooking, cleaning, tending the large vegetable garden, keeping house, and raising three boys (my two brothers followed me at intervals of five years), her real passion was music. It was music that would come to define my relationship with her. As my musical career developed, it became clear that she was living her life vicariously through mine. She had not had the opportunity to receive any formal music training. She and my father were victims of the Great Depression of the 1930s. When they should have gone on to high school, they dropped out after grade eight to work on their respective home farms. Mom also spent one year at the Winkler Bible School, shortly before she married Dad. The highlight of that year, she told me, was singing in the choir and in various trios and quartets. In later years, when I was in high school, my parents would often remind me how fortunate I was to be able to get an education.

It was much later, after my career was well established, that Mom related how she had come to acquire whatever little knowledge she had about music. There was never enough money in her family for music lessons, let alone for a piano. However, the teacher in her one-room country school offered to teach music to any interested pupils during the recess periods. There wasn't a piano in the school, but the teacher constructed a cardboard keyboard, and my mother and her classmates would learn about scales and sharps and flats and rhythm by moving their fingers about on this primitive contraption. Not having an actual sounding instrument, they would sing the notes their fingers were "playing." Arduous as this learning process must have been, it evidently worked because my mother learned to read music quite proficiently, albeit at a rudimentary level. What little skill she had she used all her life, singing alto in choirs and smaller ensembles until less than a year before her death. She also accompanied herself on the autoharp. Her determination to learn remained an inspiration to me throughout my formative years and instilled in me a sense of responsibility to make the most of the opportunities that were open to me.

The palpable delight Mom took in my musical activities was never in greater evidence than in 2006, when Winkler, having just achieved city status, celebrated the centenary of its incorporation. For the flagship concert of a weekend-long series of celebratory events, I was invited to conduct the Winnipeg Symphony Orchestra in Winkler's largest Mennonite church. My wife Maggie and I of course stayed at Mom's house, which was just two blocks from the church. The pride in Mom's eyes when she saw me walk out of the house dressed in my tails and white tie and patent leather shoes was something I'll never forget. Fifty years earlier, given the right circumstances, she too might have wished a performing career for herself. But now, a lifetime later, she was able to experience it, if only at one remove, through her son. The thought crossed my mind that at that moment she was shaking her fist at a destiny that had denied her so much. This concert—her son conducting a professional orchestra on her turf, in front of all her friends—was a crowning event for her, a sort of vindication. Just over two years later, she was gone.

My parents read extensively and were well informed. However, both of them harboured a lifelong insecurity because of their lack of formal education. That said, my mother always displayed a certain disdain for and suspicion of women who had managed to acquire secondary and post-secondary education. This puzzled me. Was it insecurity or envy, or had Mom actually come to believe the propaganda she heard from her friends and in church, namely that a woman's place really was at home? An aunt of mine had been a schoolteacher before she married my uncle. Intensely interested in all the issues of the day, she read voluminously, often at the expense of her domestic duties as a farmer's wife. My mother dismissed that intellectual curiosity as little more than pretentious claptrap. It was much later, after both women had been widowed, that they began to relate much more meaningfully and affectionately, particularly one year when they travelled together from Winkler to Waterloo, Ontario, to hear my performance of Bach's *St. Matthew Passion*.

My relationship with my mother was close and warm and affectionate. My father, a good, decent, hard-working man, was somewhat domineering and insensitive, to be sure, but always concerned about the well-being of his family. It is an understatement, however, that in my formative years my artistic inclinations failed to pique his curiosity. Not so for my mother. As my interest in music and the arts became more and more apparent, she would ask me about things I was discovering in my reading. *The Book of Knowledge*, the encyclopaedia in my country school, opened the world to me. The short biographies of the great composers especially captivated me and later, at home, I would breathlessly relate these in minute detail to my enthralled mother. And how vividly I recall the time when my teacher in the little Burwalde country school, recognizing my intense interest in classical music, took me to Winnipeg to hear the great African-American contralto Marian Anderson. The beauty, the emotion, the obvious excellence of this performance made a deep impression on me. Mom, never considering for a moment that she too might have accompanied us on that excursion, wanted to know absolutely everything about that memorable evening.

Although he came eventually to accept my passion for music and even attended a number of my concerts, my father never quite understood all of this. As far as he was concerned, music was useful, especially in church, but it was at best a luxury, a frill, having nothing to do with "real work." Moreover, both of my parents were concerned that proficiency in music could lead to the sin of pride. To his dying day, Dad remained amazed and relieved that, as a conductor and broadcaster, I actually was able to provide for my family. Mom, on the other hand, relished the fact that her first-born was heading in directions quite unconventional for other local farm boys. It was only much later, not long before his untimely death, that I came to understand that my childhood and adolescent relationship with my father had perhaps been affected somewhat by Mom's candid and, indeed, unflattering observations and insinuations. In retrospect, I see that she compared me to him, and saw in me characteristics she missed in her husband. Sigmund Freud might have had fun with that! Indeed, in the five or six last years of Dad's life, I began to see the generous, nuanced, affectionate man he really was. How I wish I had been allowed to see that side of him much sooner. But that said, it was my mom who first gave me a sense of identity and self-worth. It was she who sat with me when I practiced the piano, who took me to compete in countless music festivals, who encouraged me to pursue my dreams and ambitions.

Given that I had two younger brothers and no sisters, ours was a decidedly masculine household. Although my mother doted on her three sons (and eventually came to think she much preferred boys to girls), the fact that she craved feminine company was borne out with the appearance of Maggie, the young woman whom I would marry. My dad was proud as punch of his daughter-in-law to be; my brothers were speechless at the sight of this creature who did her hair and put on makeup. But it was Mom who soon found a kind of soulmate in Maggie. The year before we were married, I was finishing my undergraduate studies in the United States. Maggie, a student in Winnipeg, would frequently take the bus to Winkler for the weekend to spend time with my family. Those were delightful times for Mom who, accomplished seamstress that she was, insisted on sewing a new dress for Maggie each time. That dress would be given its debut outing in church the next day, Mom and Dad sitting proudly on either side of this beautiful young woman who had come into their lives. Soon it was time to start work on the wedding gown, a task my mother took on with enthusiasm and devotion. Those Saturdays in Winkler were delightful times, to hear Maggie tell it. Mom would sew, and Maggie would prepare the meals for the day. From time to time, when they both needed to take a break, the two of them would get on Dad's little Honda motorcycle, Mom perched happily behind her future daughter-in-law. One or two laps around the section, and they'd be back at their domestic chores, developing a close and lasting mother-daughter relationship.

My mother was surprisingly (or so it seems to me now, inveterate navel-gazer that I have become) unselfconscious. She would say or do things, mostly quite oblivious to how these things might be perceived or interpreted. One vignette will suffice as illustration. It was the Valentine's Day weekend; Maggie and I were officially engaged, I was a student far away, and this was another of Maggie's Winkler weekends. I had ordered a dozen roses to be delivered to her student residence in Winnipeg. They arrived after Maggie had left, so another young woman (a former high school classmate of mine, also from Winkler) offered to take them with her and drop them off at the farm. Mom had always thought this young lady and I would have made a good match. When she left the farm, having presented the roses to Maggie, Mom, clearly not realizing *what* she was saying to *whom*, said, "Ah, it's too bad ... Howard and she would have made such a good pair, especially since she's a local girl and everything would be so much simpler." Maggie was stunned to hear this from her fiancé's mother, with whom she had by now forged a very close bond. But it soon became clear to her that Mom was in fact taking Maggie into her confidence; never once did it occur to Mom that her comments might be misconstrued!

Over the years, my growing curiosity regarding our family history began to intrigue my mother as well, although sadly far too little of our past has been properly documented. Our family are so-called *Kanadier*, which is to say they came to Canada from Ukraine in the 1870s, well before the *Russländer*, who migrated to these shores in the years following World War I. In my family there was little sense of history; we led a simple year-to-year existence, maintaining only a few photographs as documentation of significant family events. Prior to my first trip to Ukraine in 1995 to explore our family's roots, Mom expressed surprise and even skepticism at my interest in our family's history. Why would I want to know about events that happened so long ago and that, by all accounts, had been hard and painful? But as I began to enquire about our family's past, she became more and more engaged, even going so far as to fill in some critical genealogical gaps. Increasingly she was deferring to my interests and opinions. While she had influenced and shaped me as a child, it now seemed that our roles were gradually reversing and she was being shaped by my pursuits and my thinking.

Although she took pride in all three of her sons (my brothers are successful in business and agriculture), it was my career as a conductor and music broadcaster that seemed to resonate most with her own proclivities. One week before she died, I hosted my final broadcast on CBC Radio (she had always been one of my most loyal listeners). I called her in her hospital room that same day, and we discussed my broadcasting swan song in great depth and detail. It was to be my last significant conversation with her.

I would be remiss if I didn't mention the importance of the Mennonite/Christian faith to my mother. She was a pious woman, careful always to emphasize the importance of faith to her sons. The church was an essential aspect of her life, social as much as religious. Hers was not a deeply probing or questioning faith, and indeed she was more than a little disturbed when my own spiritual quest took some unexpected liberal twists and turns. So it came as a great comfort to her that her first-born did, however, find spiritual refuge in the music of Johann Sebastian Bach. I shall never forget the *St. Matthew Passion* performance (mentioned earlier) she attended. A couple of days prior to the concert, I sat down and explained to her the entire complex web of symbolisms and musical techniques and theological inferences that pervade the entire work, and that continue to inspire and move me to this day. Mom was transfixed and referred to that conversation and that concert for years afterward.

There was a tension in my mother's life arising from the gap separating the realities of her life from her unfulfilled dreams, which she harboured to her dying day. It's something every artist has to endure, this element of "paradise lost." I learned from her that this is normal, something to be faced with courage, stoicism, and good humour. Although my life has been relatively carefree, there were some difficult times, when my youthful idealism clashed with practical realities. In addition to the unwavering support and profound understanding of Maggie, it was my mother's love for me—steadfast, forgiving, unconditional—that sustained me through some of those darker existential days. Mom's love was my Rock of Gibraltar; it taught me how to relate lovingly and fully as a friend, a husband, a father, and a grandfather.

If I were to summarize my mother's life, I would have to say that while she enjoyed, and indeed celebrated, her family, her church, her friends, she nonetheless felt trapped by circumstances, chiefly the Great Depression, which ended any notions she might have had about continuing her education. This resulted in a sense of marginalization, certainly a feeling of inadequacy. But she never passed that insecurity on to us. My brothers and I and our families represented the freedom and the future she never had. She didn't understand all of my decisions—going to school in the United States and then, later, in Germany; marrying a woman from far away; moving our young family away from Manitoba to Ontario; our extensive international travels—all these were strange and somewhat threatening concepts to her. But she embraced them because I was and represented everything she could never be. For that positive attitude and for empowering me with the freedom to become who I am, I am eternally indebted to her.

All women become like their mothers. That is their tragedy. No man does. That's his.
   —Oscar Wilde, *The Importance of Being Earnest*

Andrew and Mary

Reconciling Caring with Conflict: A Memoir of Mom

Andrew C. Martin

Raspy, laboured breathing broke the silence of the sterile, dimly lit room. The figure in the bed lay unmoving, unresponsive. The rhythmic rise and fall of the chest along with the accompanied intake and release of air were the only indications of life. "She won't make it through the next twenty-four hours," they said.

The clashing hospital aromas—disinfectant, body odour, fresh-cut flowers—assailed our olfactory receptors as we hovered around her bed, waiting, helpless, present. For fifty-five, fifty-three, fifty-one, forty-eight, forty-five, forty-one, and thirty-six years she mothered all seven of us. She loved us, "each one of you ... equally" she would say, emphasizing each word carefully, deliberately, her white bonnet nodding along. Our mother never tired of reminding us that we were special.

During months of deteriorating health Mom had excruciating pain, but we saw it only in her face. She did not complain about her suffering—not once. And she clung to life like she did everything else—with tenacity. As the night dragged on we reminisced, laughed, cried, and fought, but her heart would not stop beating. My brother Al made a comment with his dry, witty sarcasm; this gave rise to a reaction from my big sister, and in a replay from yesteryear she jumped up and grabbed his ear in a mock shriek.

Mom didn't move—the gravelly breathing continued as quiet settled back on the room, and each of us began to mull over our personal connection to the collective familial dynamics. Mom was holding on to the narrow cord of life with her strong inner will. I imagine that she was insisting on holding on to life, not for her own sake, but in order to continue her mothering of us.

She had nursed us countless nights; indeed, our mother was a veritable Nightingale. No matter the symptom or ailment, she had a remedy, a solution for everything. If the first treatment didn't work there were multiple other things to try. She was devoted and tender, constantly hovering when fevers, aches, and chills shook the body. When I was retching Mom was there holding the bowl with one hand, and with her other arm around me she steadied me, keeping me from falling over. But she had a harsh side to her, too.

Mary Bauman was born in 1928 on the fourth line of Peel Township several miles north of Floradale, Ontario, in Wellington County. Her Pennsylvania Mennonite pioneer ancestors arrived in Waterloo County in covered Conestoga wagons at the dawn of the nineteenth century. As land was settled and large families multiplied, Mennonites relentlessly pushed the boundaries of settlement north and west to new, cheaper farmland. Less than one hundred years earlier, the Bauman farm had been part of a vast tract of forest known as Queen's Bush, set aside for the Anglican Church.

Before the Mennonites came, the Queen's Bush offered a new beginning for escaped slaves. Nearly two thousand of these resilient pioneers lived in the Queen's Bush, making it the largest black community in Upper Canada. They established churches and schools, but due to isolation, lack of infrastructure, and unscrupulous land agents, many were forced from their land in the 1840s when it was privatized. Less than a century later in the 1930s when Mary was a young girl, there were still a few scattered black families living in the area, but more common were the "tramps." They walked up the dusty road away from the big cities looking for work in exchange for food and shelter. Some stayed for a meal and the night; others were given work. Mary was scared of some of the rougher-looking ones, but feeding them supper made her feel happy inside.

Winters were hard in those days and roads were not maintained. Only occasionally were horses and cutters able to work their way through the snow and across the fields, so visiting, shopping, and churchgoing were rare occasions. It was both a treat and a great adventure for Mary to be tucked into the cutter with her father, the stones keeping their feet warm as they set off for Ruggles General Store in Floradale. This was their link to society, to the mail and supplies. And there was always the possibility that Father would spare a penny for candy.

When Mary was a young girl she worked all summer gathering clover for her older brother's rabbits, and with her five cents' earnings she would go excitedly to Ruggles to buy one package of gum. My mom remembers how each piece individually wrapped in silver foil was chewed and saved and chewed some more, this for an entire month. In this way the single package lasted nearly a year. (This conserving spirit was passed on to us. When we were young Mom taught us to stick our gum on the side of the fridge when we went to bed at night. The next morning the gum would be hard and flavourless, but once it warmed up at least the texture came back.)

Mary's father, Isaac, was no stranger to travel and homesteading. He was born on the plains of Iowa, and before he was married he ran a steam-threshing crew that travelled across numerous farm communities. His father was Jesse Bauman, the notorious Old Order Stauffer bishop who led a group of Mennonites from Ontario to Iowa in 1887. In reaction to the threat of "worldly" influence, they sought greater austerity and simplicity in life. The strong ascetic focus on self-surrender, self-denial, humility, simplicity, obedience, and community was not unlike the medieval monastic reform movements, but this movement included the entire family. Like their ancestors, the Anabaptists, the Stauffer Mennonites desired to bring all of life into faithful discipleship in an effort to imitate the life of Christ. Despite its best intentions, however, the Mennonite community in Osceola County, Iowa, failed epically in less than three decades. Arising out of five distinct Mennonite communities, this new conglomerate never figured out how to bridge their differences. Frequently they went for long periods without Communion because of disagreement, and eventually they all moved away.

Though Jesse was the leader of a group seeking simplicity of life, when he moved from Iowa to Pennsylvania he eventually left the "Horse and Buggy" church and became a member of the most progressive wing of the Old Orders, the car-driving Weaverland group. Certainly Jesse was a complicated man, whose complexity is borne out not only in his wavering between a conservative and more liberal lifestyle, but also in his propensity to drink too much. The story goes that he even imbibed just before taking his turn behind the pulpit. That same pulpit is now on display at Muddy Creek Farm Library near Ephrata, Pennsylvania. It has a deep groove worn into it, ostensibly an imprint of Jesse's perpetually convulsing thumbnail. (As a counselling therapist, I wonder if his self-medication in the form of alcohol was a coping mechanism to allay a mood disorder.)

Jesse's son Isaac, my mother's father, was among the minority to move back to Ontario when the Iowa settlement failed. He married a Waterloo County girl, Rebecca Martin. Mary, my mother, was the fourth-born child in this family. When she was a teenager they bought a car and joined the car-driving Old Order movement. Unlike her siblings, who suffered from a rare disease that left them crippled, Mom was healthy. She was short, strong, and stout. She could also be fiery. At a young age she learned to look out for her siblings and others who needed her protection, regardless of the consequences. On one occasion, I recall her telling the story of how she turned all her childhood anger onto a pestering rooster, killing it because it would not stop pecking at her terrified younger brother. For this she received a whipping from her father.

At Mom's funeral a former classmate remembered Mom pulling her home on a wagon after she had hurt herself at school and could no longer walk. It was never a question for Mom whether to help others; she did it naturally and with passion. With fire in her eyes she would recount stories about the bullies at her school, and a particular story about a teacher who picked on one of the boys because he had a learning difficulty. She had a strong sense of justice and a soft spot for the underdog. But sadly, she had no experience or knowledge of how to bring restitution to the conflict within her own family.

Mom was twenty when she married my dad. My parents grew up in the Old Order Mennonite horse and buggy group, but were baptized and married in the Old Order black car group, the Markham-Waterloo Mennonite Conference. They subsequently joined the fledgling Conservative Mennonite movement in 1960 after more than a decade of marriage, with four kids in tow. This Conservative Mennonite movement began in reaction to the "worldly" assimilation occurring in the "Old" Mennonite Church in the late 1950s. It held as orthodoxy the theology and traditions inaugurated at the turn of the twentieth century by Bishop Daniel Kauffman. A rigorous involvement in church was part of the heritage, so our family not only went to church religiously every Sunday, but we also attended services on Wednesdays, took part in regularly held mission conferences and special Easter meetings, and were expected to be at every event connected to the annual revival meetings. Furthermore, in order to protect children from dangerous worldly influences, such as dancing and the teaching of evolution, parochial schools were founded.

In all of the Mennonite traditions of my forebears, dress served as a significant religious symbol. But in the conservative Mennonite tradition cape dresses, head coverings, and plain suits took on heightened meaning, and wearing them was taught as if it were biblical doctrine. As chief seamstress of the family, my mom's responsibility was to make sure our clothes met the requirements of the church. In this Mom was very conscientious to support the expectations and rules of the church.

In the '70s when bell-bottoms were in fashion, Mom was adamant that they were unacceptable for us, even though it meant more work for her. I remember her opening up the pant leg and narrowing its seam even as I begged for leniency. And while there was always a pile of shirts, dresses, and trousers of our own in need of repairs and alterations, Mom also made herself available to sew for others, such as the young woman who came to our church in her "worldly" clothes and needed a "cape dress" in order to fit in. In this way Mom was involved in what my brother recently dubbed a kind of "clothing evangelism."

Not everything that Mom did was motivated by religious, ascetic ideals, however. She also appreciated beauty in its varied forms. In fact Mom had a fetish-like love of hair. When we were very young she did not want our hair to be cut, and my two-year-old photos reveal a beautiful blond "girl" with shoulder-length curls. Later in life she would come running to save our "curls" from the electric clippers as Dad cut our hair. For although long hair for boys and men was anathema in our community, and Mom ostensibly supported that view, it distressed her to see our beautiful locks of hair fall to the floor. Till the day she died, Mom kept a lock of our very first curls in an heirloom teacup in the china cupboard. She could identify all seven specimens of hair though none of them was marked.

Mom's love of floral beauty was clearly on display for the local community to enjoy. Our garden was filled with row upon row of gladiolas, zinnias, snapdragons, dahlias, asters, and daisies. Surrounding the garden and our house was a continuous sea of colour, and hanging pots and urns graced the porches on the front and side of our two-storey brick home. All these flowers were raised in our greenhouses, where Mom spent a significant portion of her time, contributing to the family business. After people, family, and food, flowers brought Mom more joy than anything else. She worked tirelessly to bring beauty alive through the many plants she loved and nurtured.

Music was central to our family, and we all learned to sing in four-part harmony as a matter of course when we were children. Although Mom was not a particularly gifted singer, she loved music and helped to instill a love of music in her children. She was often the instigator of singing and would bring the hymn books and coax the family to make music together. In our family we had a ladies trio and later, when the boys got older, we had a male quartet. Both ensembles sang a cappella at numerous events, and Mom was clearly proud of her children's music ability, though it would have been unacceptable to admit it. In the evening as I was going to bed my sisters would play hymns in their bedroom on an old pump organ donated by an uncle, and Mom would hum along.

People remember Mom for her warm and generous spirit. She was not merely friendly and outgoing; she had a way of pleasing people that was extraordinary. The flowers she grew were not just for her own enjoyment. Many were given away, and even with paying customers Mom frequently undercharged. Mom taught me that there were things more important than financial gain, such as generosity and friendship. It used to embarrass me how friendly Mom would be to complete strangers, but now I cherish those memories.

Mom's generosity and friendliness were best exemplified by her habitual hospitality with regard to food and lodging. It was not uncommon to set an extra plate or two on the supper table for visitors who dropped by. When old friends from Pennsylvania needed lodging for a weekend while they attended a local church conference, Mom accepted this challenge on the spot even though it was a very large group: thirty adults. Likewise, when we brought home our friends on a Sunday after church, Mom was always welcoming even though it meant more mouths to feed. Our family hosted an annual youth group corn roast and crokinole party in our traditional Waterloo County style bank barn. What began as a one church event, after more than a decade came to include multiple churches, with more than eighty youth in attendance. Mom was a gracious hostess and never complained about all the work this event took; indeed, she loved to mingle with the youth. Being with people clearly energized her.

Family was one of the highest priorities for Mom, and she went out of her way to plan extended family events. Every Christmas our immediate family grew to include my mom's unmarried handicapped siblings. Though as kids we resented it at times, we came to realize that life was meant to be shared with others. We were taught that joy comes from doing good for others. Our Mennonite religious culture, along with Mom's outgoing nature, meant that we did what in some contexts would be viewed as pastoral work. Our family sang at nursing homes, we visited aged relatives, and we provided food and shelter for various people who needed a place to stay. Publicly, at least, our family presented itself as a religiously stable unit.

However, there was much that was hidden from the public eye. Rarely was there any meaningful agreement or long-standing harmony between my parents, and this discord spilled over into all kinds of family tensions. Growing up, my siblings and I were put in the impossible situation of listening to complaints from each of our parents about the other, which of course we were unable to do anything about. There was no physical violence between them, but the passive-aggressive emotional and psychological warfare was palpable, debilitating, and corrosive.

Our annual summer vacation was a much-anticipated trip by us children, but rather than provide a relief from the habitual familial conflict, it seemed to exacerbate it. The preparation for departure was always tense, and we all held our collective breath. The tension was primarily between Mom and Dad, but it played out in all of us in various ways as we were left to deal with their dysfunction. We could feel the tension a week before we were to leave, and as the days counted down it only got worse. Because it was summertime, Mom had innumerable tasks that she needed to complete before leaving: canning, freezing, mending, weeding, laundry, meal preparation, cleaning, and packing. She was not a well-organized person, perhaps due to her dogged perfectionism. This combination eventually resulted in fireworks.

As departure day drew nearer, Mom fussed with preparations while Dad's frustration and anxiety rose. He would stomp, bang, mutter and fume, and launch into verbal tirades about Mom's slow progress to whomever would listen. As kids we would alternatively try to protect Mom by confronting and attacking Dad, but would often capitulate and end up harassing Mom too. The entire situation was chaotic and counterproductive. The tension and anxiety gnawed at my stomach as I worried, "What if we never leave?" After Dad's self-imposed departure time had come and gone, there was still laundry to take off the wash line, dishes to dry, clothes to fold, sandwiches to make, flowers to water, carrots to pull, kohlrabi to peel. Brusque, raw, hurtful words were spoken, feelings were hurt; we alternatively retreated in silence or attacked with vengeance. Everyone was upset. But finally, after a roller coaster of emotions, we were all packed into the old Ford station wagon.

The black mood followed us out the lane and down the road, but as the miles rolled by the "cloud" lifted and the chaos was forgotten as new adventures loomed. There were many memorable family vacations. Two summers we explored the pristine beauty of northern Ontario in a rented bus converted into a camper. No matter that it was old and rustic, the novel experience of sleeping in a bunk bed, plus living in a camper, made it an unforgettable adventure. Later we travelled to the distant state of Minnesota to visit my older sister, who had married and moved there. Compared to my friends, we travelled a lot, and I bragged to them that I had swum in all five of the Great Lakes. I was proud of my family, but not all was well.

Conflict was never far from the surface. Mom and Dad could both be extremely stubborn, and often Mom was more open than Dad was to the spontaneous ideas of her children. I remember on one trip we children tried to appeal to her sense of fun and asked if we could stay at a motel with a pool. She pleaded on our behalf, knowing the joy it would bring to us boys. Communication between my parents was never particularly constructive, and in a situation like this it became tense and terse. In the end, Dad won and we did not get to swim.

In moments like those I curled up inside, devastated by my dad's lack of understanding, his lack of respect for me as a person. At the same time I felt that Mom understood my basic longings and needs. (Her insight and sensitivity are traits I would like to think she has passed on to me.) Mom's intervention on my behalf was not always present, however, and she could not protect me from all the aggression in our family. The violence in our house was not just verbal and psychological; it was also physical. I was an easy prey for my older brother's frustration, a frustration that probably stemmed from an emotionally distant dad. Being fifty pounds lighter and six years younger put me at a distinct disadvantage. As I lay pinned with my face to the floor and my arm twisted behind my back, my brother demanded that I say "uncle." I might have been small, but I was also stubborn and determined, just like my mother. I would kick and scream and, in a moment of terror and rage, I would resort to biting; I would not say "uncle," for that was to admit defeat and weakness. So when Dad came to break up the fight I was viewed as part of the problem, and could also anticipate a kick, a hit, or a punch from him. Indeed, as my brother and I headed for safety, we kept our arms over our heads to fend off the rain of his blows. Guaranteed assaults from both my big brother and my dad were a heavy burden to carry as a child, a reality that Mom could not shield me from. At the time I judged her for that. But eventually I realized the difficult situation she was a part of, and even found some limited refuge from her tender side; this brought a measure of stability to my life that I would not otherwise have had.

One of those tender moments came with the springtime thaw. Like any kid I loved to play in water puddles, the bigger the better. My cousin, who was my neighbour, had a lovely water puddle on his yard. From our young perspective it seemed like a veritable pond. It was deeper than our boots, and when we were in a hurry to get "on the water" we had to be creative and use whatever raw materials were at hand. One time, we decided to tip an old steel fifty-five-gallon drum on its side; while its buoyancy was excellent, its tendency was to roll in the water like a spinning log. We solved that problem by using old semi-buoyant rubber tires under our feet to stabilize the roll. Finally, we sat back to back straddling the drum; it was a precarious perch. We had barely reached the deep part of the "pond" when my cousin lost his footing and fell off. Like a proverbial see-saw, the drum reared up when my cousin fell off and my end went down. I slid into the ice-cold water onto my butt, submerged to my chin. My cousin and I sprang from the icy water and slogged to shore in our waterlogged clothing.

We lit out for home with a continual sloshing in our rubber boots. My cousin's house was close by, and I could hear his mother yelling at him as I fell into a hard run for my own home. I was afraid of my own mom's reaction; I was sure she would be angry with me. When she saw me, she took one look and ordered me, "Get out of your clothes and into the tub." But she didn't raise her voice, nor did she raise her hand against me. As I lay soaking in the hot water, warmed inside and out, I was grateful that this time it was Mom's nursing instincts that kicked in rather than her authoritarian inclinations.

For everyone in my family, an attempt to forget the chaos of dysfunctional relationships came in the form of reading. I was often so lost in my book that I blocked out everything around me. When Mom told me to do something, I didn't hear her. Even dinner calls were frequently "unheard" until Dad's voice thundered. This love of story I surely inherited from my mother. Indeed, it was because she read to us in early childhood that our desire to learn to read for ourselves was fuelled.

I felt warm and safe when Mom read to us. We would beg her to leave her unremitting household chores to come and open up a book with us, as we lay in bed. Once she started reading she could no more put down the book than we could stop listening, and it didn't take much convincing to have her read "just one more chapter," and then "one more." Dad would periodically report the passing of time as he hollered up the stairs, clearly making known his displeasure at the late-night reading. Eventually he would give up and go to bed by himself. Perhaps there was more that she was escaping than we knew.

Mom read us the classics of nineteenth- and twentieth-century America with titles such as: *Glengarry School Days, Little Women, Black Beauty, Tom Sawyer*; she read us the story about Harriet Tubman and all the books by pioneer author Laura Ingalls Wilder; and of course, her most adored "Anne" books. We balked at the girlish titles, but we enjoyed them all, even if we didn't readily admit it at the time. For her own reading, Mom had a penchant for the romance genre. The Christian, Grace Livingstone Hill series was too explicit in its romance for our conservative community not to consider it controversial, but Mom loved those books. She left them lying around, but even "racier" novels were kept hidden in her bedroom, under stacks of clothing or in the bottom of her dresser drawers.

But our voracious appetite for books also led to conflicts. We subscribed to the usual periodicals popular with conservative Mennonites, like those from the Amish, Pathway Publishing, but nothing was as highly prized as the *Reader's Digest*. Being the first to read the new edition was a monthly ritual that we literally fought over, and once the coveted magazine was inside our house, the fights continued. Even while we were reading it someone was liable to snatch it out of our hands if we weren't holding it tightly enough. Only begging, physical harassment of the offender, or parental intervention could resolve that problem. Mealtimes were also a problem; where to hide the *Reader's Digest* so that someone wouldn't beat us from the table and take our beloved magazine was a constant challenge. We might try to sneak it to the table and sit on it, but if Dad caught us he would confiscate it.

Running out of reading material necessitated a trip to the attic, where Mom saved every issue of all the periodicals we received, including the *Reader's Digest* all the way back to the 1950s. We happily trekked up two flights of stairs to haul down an armload of magazines, and then pore over each issue from cover to cover. We had other reading material, too. There were books on every level of our house: the attic, the upstairs, the main floor, and the basement. Many were bought at second-hand stores and at library sales. And in the winter, when work slowed down on the farm, the local public library supplied us with even more books. The librarian always looked a little shocked and amused when three or four of us would each walk out with a dozen or more books. Imagine how surprised she would have been if she knew that we often read each other's books as well. With no TV to distract us, we assumed our love of printed material was normal.

Surely a love of reading handed down to us from our mother provided a much-needed sanctuary in a house filled with conflict and contradictions. There was a rag drawer in the bathroom that was shallow but wide, and lined with neatly folded square flannelette cloths. When we got sick with a sore throat, Mom would vigorously slather our necks, chests, and backs with Vicks ointment that burned like hell and made our eyes water. Her fingers—roughened from working in the dirt and perforated from quilting and sewing—felt like eighty-grit sandpaper. Mom's concern for our health meant we got thorough attention. I felt loved when she fussed over my fevered body, but her roughness made me feel angry. Finally, with the Vicks duly administered, Mom wrapped one of her pre-warmed soft flannelette rags around my neck, and I felt soothed and comforted. (Later I found those same rags under the sink in a pail of stinky, bloody water.)

The bewildering array of feelings raised by tensions in my family was compounded by the deep guilt the church foisted on me. Revival meetings were frequently emotional affairs, with loud and forceful preaching accompanied by pulpit pounding. Riveting, sensational stories replete with dire warnings about "hellfire and brimstone" and the inevitable slow, plaintive singing of "Oh sinner come home!" were terrifying to a young child. In the silence of my bed at night I could almost hear the "weeping and gnashing of teeth," and feel the heat of flames awaiting me. I prayed a thousand repentance prayers alone in the darkness while shadows danced around the walls and creaking floors fuelled imaginations of evil beings ready to snuff out my life and send me to hell.

Conservative Mennonite teaching predictably put a huge emphasis on family, but the assumption was that "victorious" Christians didn't struggle with relationships. Surrendering one's life to God was understood supernaturally to dissipate any emotional baggage. There was no place for ongoing problematic psychological attachments. Indeed, the notion of psychology was treated with deep suspicion. Already as a child I strove to reconcile my family experience with what I was taught at church. And since I was taught that anger toward my family was wrong, I inevitably retreated into a state of guilt. And thus began another round of repentance prayers.

Coming to peace with the ambivalence I felt toward my mother due to her simultaneous caring and fault-finding nature, due to her central role in family conflict, began long before her health started to degenerate. In my late twenties I realized there was much that I did not understand about life, things that I wanted to understand. This need was central to my decision to enter academia at the age of thirty-one. At that time I had a grade-eight education, a spouse, three children, and three small businesses. Several academic degrees later, I am even more aware of the limitations of my knowledge. Yet, at the same time the occasion to reflect on God, the world, and human relationships has helped me to gain a level of intellectual and existential healing for my restless soul. As I see it now, life is a journey of reconciliation, coming to terms with ourselves in relation to all that is.

Leaving the "safety" of our conservative Mennonite community for the sake of education led my young family to a new spiritual community. Here our larger questions could be more openly grappled with. This move was difficult for my mom, and she confronted us with the common Conservative Mennonite "concern for our souls." This presented me with the opportunity to have an adult conversation with my parents that was not possible as a child or a youth. Though unable to grasp our changing theology, they offered us acceptance and love in spite of our evolving beliefs. As a result of this, I was able to forgive them for their mistakes in my childhood and youth, even though they never asked for that forgiveness.

My siblings came from afar to be with Mom in her final hours. That long night that was Mom's last, we reminisced and experienced yet again the caring and conflict that was our inheritance. Mom hung on to the slim thread of life until the following afternoon. We sang softly as her breathing slowed to a whisper and she gently slipped into another world. The tears flowed as our ears strained to hear the eternal silence.

Like Socrates, I agree that "the unexamined life is not worth living." My mother's passing from this world has given me the opportunity to ponder further her legacy to me; I believe that my mother has left me a unique inheritance. Thus it has become my life's work to identify and reconcile the conflict of my past in order to appreciate more deeply the caring that my mother gave to me and that I hope to pass on to others.

The greatest gift Mom gave me was her nurturing love; in adulthood I came to understand it as unfaltering. Rather than the "forgive and forget" indoctrination I had received from my church, I learned that I needed to remember in order to forgive. Remembering how much she had hurt me made me realize how much more I had to forgive her. And remembering how my mom hurt me helped me understand how much I carried that hurt with me and passed it on to those I loved most. This required me to ask my family to forgive me. If I am honest, Mom's perfectionism, procrastination, and judgemental attitudes are also apparent in my own life. More than anything this makes me realize I need to forgive my mother so that I can forgive myself.

Through a process of emotional healing, I have come to appreciate the many gifts my mom has given me. She instilled into me a love of learning, an excitement of turning the next page to see where the story goes. I have been blessed to follow that story to a level she could not possibly have imagined. My academic research has brought me back to my roots, focused on my Old Order Mennonite spiritual heritage with its quiet yet fervent, earthy and pragmatic simplicity and humility. Though this heritage comes with baggage, there is a profundity that flows through it, and my mother is a huge part of that profound heritage.

Lloyd and Elsie

Queen of Clubs*

Lloyd Ratzlaff

Mayday! Our mother's neighbour calls to say that Mom looks bad, very bad; she's been out making a garden, but something has gone awry and an ambulance is coming to take her to the Rosthern Hospital. By the time we drive out from the city, she's strapped in an emergency room wheelchair, moaning *Ohh, ohh*, lifting hands alternately to her forehead, or gripping the chair's edge and straining to get out. Her eyes seem to see, but she doesn't respond to us, and we can only repeat the things we most want her to know: *We love you; please try to rest; everyone is helping; things will be all right*—and try to believe this last utterance ourselves.

The doctor on duty arranges a transfer to Saskatoon's Royal University Hospital. I ride with Mom in the ambulance, and she calms somewhat; but at the new emergency ward she rears and thrashes

---

* Previously published in *Backwater Mystic Blues* in 2006 by Thistledown Press, Saskatoon, Sask. Reprinted with permission.

again, jabs her feet through the bedrails as if determined to get up and leave. Eventually a CT scan shows bacteria from an ear infection eating through the mastoid into the meninges between her skull and brain, and already spreading into the right temporal lobe. Air pockets generate internal pressure and make her head ache ferociously. No one will estimate the brain damage without neurological tests, and she's not conscious enough to respond.

At eighty-five, our mother still claims never to get tired but for some occasional eye strain; she maintains her own acreage, walks easily ten or fifteen kilometres a day, and keeps a calendar so full that we can't necessarily see her when we want to. She's dubbed "Mother Theresa of Laird": chauffeur for the immobile, cook and deliverer of meals, pianist for church and community events, babysitter for kids who call her Grandma Elsie—in another day she might have been labelled hyperactive, and we hope this lifelong dynamism will aid her now. Finally she settles for the night, but next morning is "combative" again—strange accusatory word for someone said to be unconscious—and it takes three nurses to subdue and medicate her.

We siblings are confounded by specialists coming and going, and in the first two days are asked half a dozen times whether we want Mom resuscitated "if something should happen." Yes, we say—until we know more, how can we say otherwise? They predict that her hearing will be gone, though some may return if she survives. Her memory and other cognitive functions (but which ones?) will certainly be affected. Some doctors are resolved to prepare us for the worst; others confine themselves to statistics: a certain percentage of similar cases die, a few recover fully, and in between are disabilities ranging from minor to severe.

We stare at Mom across the bedrail to see whether she's still breathing, as she once stood beside our cribs, and we did at our own children's: *Are you still here?* Her head turns, her eyes open, and we think *She's back!* but in the next instant we see differently—there is no recognition. Three antibiotics flow through plastic lines into her deranged body. Finally the white blood cell count drops slightly, and we hope it means the infection is contained. Days and nights begin blurring together. We practically live at the hospital, to be there if she wakes up, there if she dies.

Near the end of the week, her eyes snap to attention; scan, stop, follow our faces. She swallows and half smiles. Where she had measured seven on the coma scale (fifteen being "awake"), now she reaches ten, and maintains the level for a day. Propped up in bed, she's particularly wide-eyed as we play a tape of her favourite music. Then again, the eyes are blank—but where has she gone?

On Mothers' Day weekend, the seizures begin. Her upper body convulses, one arm jerks erratically, her face contorts, and she breathes in laboured gasps. Each spasm lasts a couple of minutes, and in the intervals she sleeps, making loud exasperated sounds. A dozen doctors are involved now with this "unusual case." Meningitis is more common in children, they say, yet not many elders have our mother's stamina. But one physician repeats several times, "She's very sick, very sick."

While the nurses suction, pummel, and turn her, I walk through the basement of an old hospital wing, into a cramped tunnel I didn't know was here. Gigantic pipes crowd my head, and signs warn of asbestos. Every so often a dark cubicle appears on the left, its shadows shifting as I approach—another stairwell to the College of Medicine above. A single playing card, the Queen of Clubs, lies on the floor. I pick her up and ascend from the tunnel, and emerge in a corridor where signs on offices advertise the specialties of each medical worker.

I sit in a lounge and stare out at the grey buildings, grey clouds. Not a doctor here on the weekend; only a distant pair of footsteps slapping the clean tiles, and the hum of Coke's big upright machine. I miss the old red icebox in Don's store when I was a kid, pulling up stubby glass bottles and snapping off the caps—*Pffttt*—on the recessed opener, frosty drops spilling to the wooden floorboards.

By the next day Mom's seizures last five minutes apiece; on the coma scale she sinks to four, and a note on her chart reads, "Does not respond to pain." We speak tenderly in her ear: *We're here with you, Mom. You're always in our hearts.*

The seizures become continuous, with rare half-minute reprieves, and they are reclassified grand mal. Three new medications are administered; one after another they fail, and the wreckage escalates. A seventh, phenobarbitol, leaves her quiet, chest rising and falling rhythmically. We keep repeating, *We love you; please don't be afraid.* Or we recite Psalms: *Yea, though I walk through the valley of the shadow of death, I will fear no evil....*

At the beginning of the second week, the hospital's senior neurologist takes five minutes to "see" their meningitis patient, and relays a message through the nurse: "Give mama a Valium drip and let her go." Within an hour, a palliative care team arrives to discuss moving her to St. Paul's Hospital. We children grope in the thick mist between "active treatment" and "provision of comfort." We look up the word *palliate*: "to reduce the violence of a disease." We don't want our mother beat up any more; she's fought the good fight. A miracle can happen, we suppose, on the west side of the river as well as here, among researchers and interns.

Around midnight a bed becomes available, and Mom's inert body is transported to St. Paul's. All medications will be reduced or withdrawn. She lies now at the mercies of a new and exceptionally kind staff, looking indeed as if she has gone to still waters and green pastures. I try to see everything twice—once for Mom, once for me.

But these workers with the sick and the dying, do they find it any easier to die themselves?

Third week. Mom runs a fever during the withdrawal, and a few mild seizures recur. Our nuclear family dysfunctions flare into the open—our fear and rage, the sad orphanages of our minds. We all need palliation. We take turns sleeping on a pullout as the oxygen hose bubbles at the head of Mom's bed, and try to recall her face without this mask, a face that met us at the door laughing, *Ha ha ha, this is great!*, that whirled in and out of rooms, *Boy, we're having a good time!*

Then, near the end of May, a bodily resurrection begins. Mom clears her throat and sneezes. Her lip curls. She opens her eyes and blinks. Wiggles the fingers of one hand, and squeezes ours. She murmurs at the rainbow beyond her window; shakes her head at the sight of a flower, "Oh, isn't that beautiful!"—the words come out clear as a bell tone.

Over the next few days, she enters our world and leaves it again, much as we go in and out of our dreams. One side of her body is paralyzed, but she smiles most of the time she's awake, new eyes flashing blue in the south window's light. Or she startles and puzzles, and quickly turns happy again. I read aloud from her old diary:

May 10, 1937– Washed and planted potatoes, and ask incredulously, "You washed dirt *off* the potatoes before putting them *in* dirt?" and she giggles like a kid.

I look across the room at her, and she forms her mouth into an O, and extends her tongue like a birdling. I give her a few drops of water and she says, "Thank you for all your help." I weep; she strokes my face with the one hand that moves. My mother is a re-born child; and she's an elder embodying gratitude, joy, serenity—God grant me such serenity. Her face looks younger than it did at Easter, when she hosted her tribe and led us in singing the doxology as we sat at her table, and consumed the meal too hastily.

One day we hear that Kathy and Abe, Mom's neighbours who had placed the *Mayday* calls at the beginning, are coming to visit the hospital. They've already tended to her garden and mowed her acreage without being asked. I tell Mom that we'll get a thank-you gift on her behalf, and though she can't speak just then, a tear forms in her eye and falls to the pillow.

As I return from my errand, the westering sun lights up Twentieth Street from end to end. There's been new rain, and the world is as green as creation day. I park near the hospital again. At the front door, on a sturdy concrete base, Jesus with open arms welcomes me.

A Catholic statue never looked so good.

* * *

The next six months are volatile for our mother. Rapid changes—some heartening, many oppressive—transform her from the lively creature she had been, to a shut-in devastated in mind and body. After further shuttlings around emergency wards and hospitals and assessment units, with a legion of experts doing as they would, Mom has settled, finally, in her room in a nursing home.

Settled? She's locked there, with a mind that goes whither and hence, and a body that sits or lies as the attendants place it, and often in great pain, this body that till the *Mayday* hardly knew what to do with its steam.

She hears and understands, even the medical people agree; but she is largely paralyzed, and the meagre speech left after the meningitis attack slowly deserts her now. Occasionally a clear phrase escapes—*Hey, mister!* she calls when the doctor comes around, and there's the odd moment of levity, at least for us, when she protests: *Oh for pete snakes!* But many of her remaining words—*yes, no, thank you*—are there unfaithfully, along with a few erroneous names by which she calls relatives and friends alike. Sometimes we infer her meaning from the bright smiles she still musters, or from her tears when she despairs of being understood.

I visit her often, feel sad and negligent when I don't, though I'm helpless to add an hour to her life or subtract one minute of pain. Whether I sit with her over a meal, or keep late-evening vigil, it comes to the same thing: not enough. I wheel her around the hallways in a Broda chair, once in a while kiss the back of her head—the drugs have made most of her hair fall out—and park in the sunniest lounge I can find, try to get a grip, and repeat what Wally at the palliative ward said the dying (and who isn't?) long to hear: *I love you. Please forgive me. I forgive you. I'll be all right.* Or we sit quietly in her room and commune by candlelight, our tears and silence more profound anyway than words. And yet, when the queen of clout reaches out the one semi-functional arm in a crook to "hug" her son, it's a benediction no old-time religion ever gave.

Pascal said that most human problems stem from an inability to sit by ourselves in our rooms. But Mom's "cure" is too drastic, while I still go too fast and without knowing where. I drive from the nursing home in her car, which I use these days, and turn up a blues album on the stereo—*Damn right,* somebody wails, *you damn right I've got the blues.*

How dumb the stuffed bunny hangs by a thumbtack on the wall of my mother's room. How bare the prairie stretches around her empty house in the late November afternoon.

Michael and Hilda

Malaver

Michael Goertzen

Outside the unlit kitchen, where we—my mother and I—stood, a manicured garden was. Along the fence a diminishing patch of tomatoes and raspberries and distant summer skies. White blossoms from the magnolia had withered some months ago. Wisteria wound slower and the Asiatic maple trembled. The hosta stood slouched along the rigorously edged lawn. A garden lamp lay on the short grass, knocked over by a trio of ring-eyed troublemakers. Reminded of the cedar—topped and covered now in Virginia creeper. Its upper three-quarters had fallen towards the kitchen, scattering conversants from this exact table but twenty years back. The tree hadn't broken through, impaled or hurt anyone. Only rumpled the eaves during some evening between that age of fire and this of hydrangea. When things didn't wait for approval, but barged in over dark rocks before shorelines could fade.

My mother was stabbing red boiled beets with a fork and peeling the skin off. She performed this with a chopping blade, towards herself, contrary to the way my father advised. It was much too late for a review of the safety regulations in the house; shingles had damaged sight nerves and left her with a fully dilated right pupil. She would cover it with her hand while focusing her gaze. Or put a sticker over one side of her glasses if she watched TV. I mentioned my appreciation for the red root began with a bowl of Ukrainian beet borscht I'd eaten in East Vancouver at a friend's some time ago. She murmured interest and said the sorrel in the planter pot beside the porch was ready if I wanted to make summa borscht. I'd need to wash it first. She said that Sandra had hired four cleaners for her house for a period of two hours. I wondered how much that totalled. Four cleaners, two hours. She hadn't asked, seemed out of place. She recalled how the rains spilled from the Buenos Aires heavens, flooding Calle Malaver. In March, hot wind crushes up against cold masses of air carried down from the Andes, causing a sudden downpour. She remembered their Volkswagon Beetle lifting up and floating down the street. Cars can float? I asked. Ours could, she replied. Isn't a car too heavy? I guess not, she said. A couple days later my cousin-in-law verified that Bugs have a kind of bottom, making them buoyant. Red juice ran in rivulets down her hands along her wrists. She put the knife down and flexed her red fingers. The currents aren't running like before, she said, meaning the sensations in her digits. You're all thumbs now, I joked. Something like that. I'm hoping it comes back. The lost motor skills. A truant car in another's yard. A little girl in a smudged dress.

My mother was raised in Olivos, the same neighbourhood Adolf Eichmann hid in for a number of years before the Mossad got him on Garibaldi. How significant is this really? An inverse retribution for anti-German sentiment in her parents' Ukraine? Even so, that Eichmann lurked around her corners adds lustre to the sway of the eucalyptus along the tracks leading the working class downtown to Retiro. She told me her friend pointed at the *Buenos Aires Herald* one day in 1960 and said, that man on the front page used to come to our house for dinner. Does that mean that my mother crossed paths with one of the twentieth century's most banal humans? Could a touch from a pant leg allow infinitesimal transference of evil? What of a glimpse through a passing car window? I daresay not. The spirit she exuded would refuse infiltration or subjugation. Between the ages of five and eleven, my mother lived a life so carefree, unregulated, and curious, any Eichmann would have frowned to see her whip past on her bicycle or lunge noisily toward the shelf of *caramelos* at the local store. *That girl with wheat-blown hair, eyes and eye teeth catching each ray.* That's what they thought of her in Olivos in the 1950s.

To use the word "raised" is inaccurate. Not how her two teenage siblings had been raised. Each given seven and nine years more, respectively, with their father. My mother was five when he died of a heart attack, disappearing early from her childhood. Some say an owl called his name in the evenings leading up to his death, and over those last days, he continuously swore, I'm going to shoot that bird. Because he never got his hands on a gun, my mother received less of him than her brother and sister did. And what about her mother? I've never asked, exactly, but I get the sense that she was worn down. Food, money, death, other concerns.

She too had come out of the Russian civil war bodily unscathed and, for that, the penance of memory had been exacted. Survivor guilt. She, like some Mennonite Iphigenia who, because it is the price of a god, must shuffle through the rites of history and the storied striations of a far-off land. In a silent struggle, she grappled with her own Anabaptist traditions, songs, and those abandoned farms of the Molotschna Colony and other communites where she and her ancestors had lived. In conjunction with their dogma and lost way of life, she brushed against Tatars and Ukrainians who had stories of what she'd thought was her and her father's Crimea. It's not implausible to say the absurdist writings of Nikolai Gogol crossed arms with the anarchy of Nestor Makhno, and Kazimir Malevich's denunciation of reason and the defamiliarization of Viktor Schklovsky kicked their legs in a most non-Mennonite manner—all occurring within the same proximal area and distilled to an atomic point around 1917. Did she recognize the dance? That the radiation from these ideas had merit, contrary to the community's beliefs, stirred, unknowingly, in her being, whether she wished for unknowing or not. And though only hundreds of Russian Mennonites were killed during that time of transition and escape—unlike an estimated 30,000 to 60,000 in the pogroms of the same time and place—who is to say how the vortices of aching memory settled in my mother's mother? So it stood to reason that besides the attendance of somnambulant caregivers, my mom was allowed the dream of many a child: to absorb the environs on one's own terms. To learn by instinct. Full immersion into imagination. It was as much as any gaucho on a bicycle could long for.

You were sitting, I hope, she said to me when I returned from the washroom. An exploding firework going off in her good eye. She shook out the last drops of olive oil over the dark red beets. What's the obsession with sitting? I wanted to know. Even into adulthood, whenever I came home, the anatomic rights of males were taken from me. It's more hygienic, she replied, logically. You aren't the one cleaning up after yourself. You don't either, I retorted. Becky Harder does that for you. (Becky Harder came in twice a month to vacuum and do the bathrooms.) Well, you know the sound disgusts me, she admitted, peeing splashes, and she added some Low German adverb. When I had my run of Olivos, there was a house up the street from Malaver, up the street that crossed near our place. Two men lived there. I forget their names. They were very kind to me. They let me play with their cat. Gave me lemonade in the summer. A neighbouring man once intercepted me before I could get to their door and asked why I always went there. I couldn't answer. These men *son peligrosos* and *son raros* and I needed to promise him I'd stay away. The way they lived was *demasiado loco*. They were probably gay when she thought about it now, she said. The neighbour then pressed some pesos from his pocket into my hand. A bribe, she called it. But really the only fault was the location of the bathroom in their home. I could hear it from the living room while watching TV. Or if I was in the backyard the window was always open. And through it I could hear that toilet in use. A receptacle receiving. One of them was always in and out of there. Alternating torrents of urine gushing into the bowl. Those disturbances echo back at me each time I hear someone peeing. It's why I can't stand the sound to this day. And why there is an X'd-out boy-standing-peeing placard nailed above the toilet. Whether or not my mom kept her promise not to return, I've forgotten. I do however know she won't want that anecdote repeated, blurry as it is.

On a subsequent day—or was it before?—I sat at the kitchen table and unfolded the paper. The front page claimed that "Duffy reaches out to 'daughter' via Facebook." The article spoke of bribery and missing fathers. Karen Duffy Benites from Lima, Peru, said the following about Mike Duffy:

> Not having him as a father or not having him recognize me as his daughter has left an emptiness in me, something only people who don't have a parent know what it feels like and what it means. It is a circle that never closes.... His response, acknowledgement, or a call will suffice. But primarily, I want him to recognize me, legally, as his daughter. I was not born from earth, air or water. I have a father. And that father is Mike Duffy. That is my right.*

In Ms. Duffy Benites' words, I heard my mother's call, though not as wild or playful. Yet it too made the sound of one remembering stories that were taken away.

Another time I came back again to Rosedale and to our family home nestled in the inner elbow of Mt. Cheam where my mother convalesced upstairs. I pushed open the bedroom door to the acrid smells of a patient. I'd been warned that Mom was in a bad physical state; I'd heard the order of events clinically relayed. Chemotherapy for non-Hodgkins lymphoma had compromised her immune system. Shingles had taken the opportunity to set up shop in her body. As the scales fell from her hair, the virus bore into her brain to fracture nerve ganglia. On a self-imposed work leave, my father assisted how he could, softening this many-mirrored disease. Nights she stood over the sink in a shudder, my father holding her, splashing her with water to keep her from passing out. Weeks she lay in darkness, on high doses of morphine and gabapentin, listening to recordings of classic literature. It was all she could do. *The Count of Monte Cristo. Max und Moritz. Heidi.* Each chapter read by a different reader. Each reader with a different accent. At first, she said, I couldn't get used to it. The person had a thick way of speaking. Then, after the next one, I began, slowly, to understand. They were all these old stories I'd heard before. In my childhood. Some of them

---

* Josh Wingrove, "Lawyer for Peruvian woman says he heard from Mike Duffy." *The Globe and Mail*, July 23, 2014.

in German. Each story was given back to me when I heard it again. Your dad read to me, too. Still does.

As minutes pass between paragraphs, memory repeats, perspectives shift, and I turn the same doorknob at the top of the same stairs and ease wide the umber spear of light. She is propped up in bed against a few pillows and her eyes are closed. The worst has passed. I take her hand and she rambles a little. The drugs blend her syntax within itself. She makes statements I don't really understand except that my dad is "such a lovely teacher man," though he hasn't taught in twenty-five years. I can see that she is in the midst of an internal trial. She is stepping out of this world and this is my own reckoning. Or so melodrama moves me to think. Her language and her body no longer conform to the structures I admire: rationality and health. Things go their own way. Raccoons knock over garden lamps. Fathers leave before children are ready. Children cross paths with hapless devils. There are matters of decorum to uphold. One falls from former temples of cedar and is chainsawed for firewood. These shoulders of stone are not stood upon, but rearranged for new preferences. Chopped beets are garnished to particulars of taste. The right ingredients are most often already there, with little control, they just build their way down. "What is it all worth?" indeed. This question, like some final honesty to pin to what we strive toward: gainful employment, evolved personality, innovative new medicine. Goals appear barbaric and scatter when a momentarily squeezed hand is the concentration of this descent.

It is perhaps to this view that my mother forces her eyes open to look upon me. Her right pupil fully contracted, resistant to the brown bulb leaking from the bedside lamp. The eye's relationship with optics runs conversely to my mom's thoughts about it, or what nature has patterned. Even if we aren't, her eye at least is ready for smaller outward tokens, like stars' light years draining past, and the ever-widening scope of what lies behind among rocks tangled in white fog. For a moment, within the sphere of her wondrous owl eye, I think I see her again in the kitchen. She is peeling beets recklessly towards herself. Outside, through the kitchen windows in variegated levels of disrepair, is the garden.

For Hilda María.

Two Poems

Introduction
I should mention that the poems "an asphodel's day card" and "between asphodel, pollen and bee" are part of a larger cycle entitled *Mosaic*. This collection, as a whole, is about people I value, places I move between, historical and genealogical associations, and daily random information. The fragmented sentences are an attempt to create something like the ancient mosaics housed in Turkey, where I now live. Also, I have removed many prepositions and replaced them with commas. At a textual level, substitution of the comma could be seen as the missing tesserae, or tiles, often apparent in mosaics displayed in Gaziantep, Antioch, and Istanbul. The comma can also represent the spaces between one piece of glass or river stone and another. Through this method, I see syntactical meaning collapse or obscure as so happens with memory. On lucky occasions, understanding of recollection can expand and become—though reinvented—poignant again.

Where is my mother in this? Mom has always been fond of flowers. They grow in her paintings, her garden; she doodles them on scraps of paper while on the phone. Certain flowers radiate life, as does my mom. I suppose that is why she is a flower here. To use another name besides her given one is a way of making sense of what I don't understand. In part, another name questions identity and recalls it as we age. As circumstances separate us, as lengthening memory divides us from past experience, reinvention and new symbols become a need.

So I remember: in the tesserae of my own childhood, I ran from fireworks on Canada Day and she found me in a cluster of elms where together we recited Psalm 23. When I had an earache, she rocked me on that old rocking chair late into the spaces of the night. It seemed she held everything in my world to herself, and the promises of loosening grip were only a whisper.

AN ASPHODEL'S DAY CARD

*the far wrote, a hand from where I stood,
applied stem cells to worn tongues, a few
affectionate words, bruised fruit, nice enough,
you and I and a love in some order, saccharine
overbearance, a fulfilled quota, never uttered
at all.*

*a propped up sideways hardened pulp, white
telescoping A or V, zygotic scars of missed
calls, my skype jana sied, some have known,
others not a chance, a glimpse of shine
through reflecting highrise glass, candle light,
bedside lamp, seeing we've remembered you,
the many times of a life, infer magnitude,
riding the crane up, it is gone.*

*artists imagine the enormity of a page, the
ephemeral Mt Cheam ridgeline, the historical
smoke signal, the embryonic crash site, your
here, the eternity of an old rocking couch, its
floral neglect of brownish, you standing in the
comedy, leant over reading, a candy-red robe,
lymphoma prize-fighter of morning light,
projections of self upon self, absorbing
substitution, inexpressible silence,* I truly am at
a loss for words, *a card says, raised, opened,
read, completion achieves each, held.*

BETWEEN ASPHODEL, POLLEN AND BEE

*I want to hold it all in, disallowing words, fall
out, forced to speak, finding a proper name for
you, something in keeping, a consistency of
anonymity, something syrupy, airborne drift,
transliterative purple, nothing fits better than
mom, mother, what I know, these terms know
who you are, that's why the phone is
constantly ringing, your inbox full, I can't go
with Dilha, too close to Gilda, honourable
names, their own right, rereading Hopkins,
rooting out the timed spring quote, for you, it
is in that season, a particle, your essence,
captured, a bit of pollen on bumblebee fur
ruffled among, in between each bloom, a daily
circuit, hive and God's creation, now a wing
seems torn, you plummeting, a jet falling over
borders, all sides, conflicted by truth of events,
unexpectedly, in accordance, history, there is
still no forbearance from these flowers you've
moved through, your life through, others kept
their edge, you your spring, the belief, the best
will float, rise even, all hold to the same, not an
avant garde camera angle, a Hollywood film, a
progressive use, fragmentary sound, a chart
topper, your mosaic, the way I've seen it, all my
life, is there anything more frustrating than
rewriting an email which has been
accidentally deleted?*

*the asphodel releasing, the pollen carried, the
carrier, pollen, you are, this process,
somewhere in the Picasso quote, he compares
everything existing with that which may,
somewhere in Hopkins expressions, beauty, joy,
God, wonder, these moments before CVP-R, I
hear you, my mother, bouquet servings of
vivacity, somewhere in dad's concern for, your
discomfort, his tears, his empty side, the bed,
virtually, all his memory, you, you are the
phrases overcoming the burn of sterile
naming, cyclophosphamide, vincristine,
prednisone, rituximab.*

*look, asphodel, look at the stars, look, look up
at the skies, o look at all the fire-folk sitting in
the air!**

---

* Gerard Manley Hopkins, "The Starlight Night," *Poems* (New York: Oxford University Press, 1948), 70.

Patrick and Margaret

I Give a Rip

Patrick Friesen

My mother used to tell me a story about losing me in a department store in Winnipeg, but I have no memory of that event. Another time, she said, I was standing beside her at the back door. She was distracted for a moment, and when she looked back I was gone. She immediately thought I had been taken and she had been left behind. The Rapture. A moment later she saw corn leaves moving in the garden, and she knew I was there, amongst the cornstalks. She hadn't known how fast a kid could move. Going lost, a life of going lost.

And, yet, despite this life of going astray, I was, and still am, deeply connected to this woman. Perhaps I was a mama's boy; certainly I was never as close to my father (though, with age, I've recognized a deep male connection, something outside ethnicity and religion). Always she had mischief in her, in her love of trickery, of puns, and of turning things around when least expected. She taught me to read before I went to school. I absorbed her love of books, her curiosity. Books were a natural life. In a photo from childhood someone gave me a few years ago, I am standing in the snow beside a couple of cousins. I have on the compulsory toque, am wearing a duffle coat, and am not looking at the camera. I'm reading a book, another one stuffed into a coat pocket. The photo reminded me that I always had a paperback jammed in a pocket, reading whenever nothing else was going on. My mother's influence.

My mother and I had our arguments, most of them having to do with religion. By the time I was twelve or thirteen I was uneasy about the belief I was being brought up in. While it took a while to formulate my disagreements, and to begin moving toward my own notions of what it was to exist on earth, my back was up by the time I reached my teens. With Father it was a simple confrontation, and puzzlement. He saw dark and light, with me being the dark undoubtedly. He didn't have much flexibility when it came to matters of religion and discipline. As he didn't have much of an education, wasn't born with an inclination toward language (for him English was pretty much a third language after Low German and High German), I had an early advantage. I would argue with him about religious matters or politics, sophistry and logic hard at work, until he grew utterly frustrated. He would throw one hand up, anger on his face, and head into the basement or, in the summer, walk outside to squat among his gladioli until he calmed down.

Mother would listen, however, sometimes argue, and often discuss. Or she'd leave the subject altogether and bring in an emotional ploy, like wondering whether I knew how my ideas hurt other people. The old martyrdom technique. But she wouldn't walk away, and I never doubted her love. I think now that she was a courageous woman, and she had a lot more openness than I encountered with most people in my hometown. She would change her mind sometimes, or modify her stance a little. This was especially true when she met someone who occupied a position different from hers. She could accommodate beliefs based on personal contact. She was always engaged, even when it hurt her. She never abandoned me. Well, maybe once.

What made our relationship what it was? In an obvious way, we were connected by age. She was hardly a generation older than me. I was born when she was twenty and, according to stories, she had not yet learned how to cook a proper meal. Father taught her the fundamentals. She told me how her first baked buns were hard as stone. And when she was entering labour in her first pregnancy, it was Father who explained to her what would happen. When she asked how he knew all this, he said it was what happened with cows on the farm; Father had that kind of earthy pragmatism. Mother responded with laughter; her laughter was always part of it. She was insatiably curious and had the mischief of the trickster in her.

She wasn't born near a crossroads or on the door's threshold, but the train did run by her backyard. My mother told me stories of climbing to the top of boxcars and running the full length of the standing train, leaping from car to car. In this picture I find her. The curiosity, the attraction to danger, and the romantic framing of life. Even today, at eighty-seven, she loves to drive to the tracks a few miles from her home just to watch and listen as the trains pass. She loves the sounds. And, she always waves and receives a return wave. I think the train, for her, represents a journey to some beautiful land, a land she has never quite ventured to find. A land she doesn't want to sully by actually travelling there physically, a land of the imagination. Recently, my brother tells me, when they stopped to watch a passing train, she said, "It's going to where my dreams are."

When she was younger she had a wonderful soprano singing voice. She sang around the house, and she sang me to sleep with Irish and Scottish ballads. She named me after one of the ballads, "The Ballad of Sir Patrick Spens." Sometimes, while doing dishes together, she and Father would harmonize. I occasionally wonder if she might have gone into a singing career if she'd been born somewhere else to a different people. Our Mennonite community did not encourage art, or individual performance. Again, that sense I had of other places, other things to do. Out of this comes a quiet longing and curiosity. Out of this comes my own journey.

Her curiosity is still active. It's an unbroken thread that ties her to youth and childhood. She shared a lot of my childhood with me, not only as a mother. She would read the same books I did, and we'd talk about them, books about the Old West and pioneers. She would sometimes be part of the games I played, or be nearby watching. Always I sensed her participation or her desire to participate. Playing baseball, I half expected her to lift her skirt above her knees with one hand and come running onto the field. It was as if she became a child along with me. It was useless time, not contributing to work, to an economy; it was time away from "the shackles of toil." From her I learned the value of childish time, useless time; I came to understand I should never lose this or I'd become another drone in the working world. She was the same with my children. I remember her, well into her fifties, taking them to her rural property in winter and camping out in a tent.

When my son was four or five, my mother was playing some game with him at her land outside town. He climbed a poplar, clapped his hands over his eyes, and said, "You can't see me." She immediately accepted this logic. Of course if he couldn't see her, how could she see him? And she kept looking for him. I suspect she wasn't simply accepting his logic; it was, to some extent, her own logic. If she can't see something, can't understand, then probably it doesn't exist. She has implicit trust in her immediate, physical experience. For her, generally, there doesn't seem to be a point in speculating about something that isn't.

I have memory of that connection, that bridge between me as child and mother as child-adult. With her I didn't need to fully encounter the adult world with its caution, its limiting instructions, and its failure of memory. I think my childhood was extended by her. As Traherne wrote, "how like an angel came I down," so I remained longer in the angel realm than I would have with another mother.

This may be her fundamental influence on me, on the fact I became an artist. There was no talk of this, no expressed ambition, only a life lived in the immediacy of raw existence. Only later did the adult world of "must" and "should" enter; only later was I taught that there were absolute beliefs I had to accept, even if the beliefs flew in the face of what my actual experience showed me.

I was puzzled by the inconsistency between her adult beliefs and what she accepted in childhood. Later, I came to understand that her religious beliefs had been somewhat hardened by the church she joined upon marrying my father. Father, himself, had a role in this. He was a serious man who, after having run away from his birth family for a year, riding the rails, working in threshing gangs, returned as a born-again Christian. He returned as a man of deep integrity, but also as a Christian who believed he had to give up things he loved "too much." If he loved something very much it might come between him and God. He gave up the guitar, for one thing. He limited his love of hockey by attending very few games. He imposed this limitation on me as well. I wasn't allowed to pursue hockey, or baseball, beyond the first few years of participation. I remember turning to him, standing on a snowbank behind the side boards of an outdoor rink, after I had scored a goal. I saw him face away, not applauding; in fact, he pretended not to have seen. He didn't want to encourage my love of sports. I learned not to turn toward him.

Mother was not like that. If Father accepted what he saw as the dictates of God, she was more likely to stand at the gate between God and human, mediating. She had a joy in things, sometimes an unusual joy. After returning from Philadelphia, where she had travelled to see her oldest brother receive his PhD, she told me she hadn't enjoyed watching the Phillies and Milwaukee Braves game nearly as much as one of my Little League games. I asked why. "Because, when they hit the ball high into the outfield in the big leagues you know they'll catch it, so it's not very exciting." She much preferred our youthful flawed games; she loved improvisation.

So, what am I unravelling here? Trying to understand this woman for who she is, who she was, I am doing an end run around an adult religious system. For me it seems this fundamentalist teaching was a layer laid on top of the free spirit I knew. A unique spirit, certainly, but also a spirit that came partly from nurture, primarily from her father, a quiet, intelligent man who loved settling in front of a canvas in his basement, a glass of wine nearby, and painting landscapes. He was a compassionate man free of rigid thinking. Like him, and my mother, I want something I know in my body, something in my blood, not some abstraction that hardly touches memory, that disappears so easily.

Going back, my mother's grandmother, Anna, was a foundational influence on her, and through her on me. Great-grandmother Anna had committed the scarlet sin within her community. Though this made her an outsider, it didn't diminish her at all. With an admirable inner strength she brought up her son, my grandfather, without looking back. She passed on her compassion, possibly a compassion born of her own vulnerability. She was a storyteller, a mythmaker, and she was undoubtedly a trickster. Turning things on their heads was one of her traits. Her grandchildren adored her. This single woman, this old woman, who lived next door to her son and his family, who left gifts for them in the hollows carved in the snow around trees. Always she had a story about how the gifts got there, or what mythical character had brought them.

As a young mother Anna washed the floors of the town hall and other public buildings; she also did laundry for various women in town. Her house became a meeting place for both well-off and poor women. And whatever she had was easily given away. My mother remembers a woman praising Anna for the dress she was wearing. A little later Anna disappeared into her bedroom, coming out with the dress wrapped in paper, and giving it to the woman who had admired it. This was, apparently, not unusual in her home.

Anna's son, my grandfather, was similar though not quite as radical. I knew him for his generosity, his unjudging acceptance of all humans, and his sly, self-deprecating, and often pomposity-puncturing humour. I knew him as a gentle man standing in his garden leaning on a hoe, smoking a cigarette. Mother told me that when she came home late from her friend's house, and it was dark, her father would be sitting on the front porch singing so that she knew where home was. She remembered "Old Black Joe" guiding her, her following the song, her father's voice. Out of this came my mother. Out of smoke drifting skyward, out of songs, stories, and tricks.

From her father and grandmother she inherited a love of story and myth. Without a drop of Scottish blood, she was a woman of the heather, though never really wanting to actually travel there. She sang folk songs, Scottish, Irish, even Russian. She sang me into a Celtic sleep many nights. Or, she played the piano in the living room, having left the door to my bedroom slightly ajar. The one song I recall is "Träumerei" by Schumann. I travelled many places at night.

Her stories of the old days (*Fräjoah*) may have been true, probably were. But they have become myth to me. She told me she was standing near the screen door at the back of the house during a thunderstorm when she was a child. Suddenly, a ball of fire whirled up against the screen door. It was lightning, spinning, she said. Many years later, I woke to see a buzz saw of fire spinning with a serrated edge in the corner of my room. This time it was the spirit of my dead father letting me know he was gone and wouldn't be back; he was no longer a father, son, husband, brother, nothing but spirit.

She told me Gypsies would travel through her town in southern Manitoba every year. One evening they camped just outside town, their caravans in a circle. She sneaked as close as she could, saw their tethered horses and a campfire in the middle of the circle. I don't remember any more of the story than this, or perhaps she never told more. It's an image I've lived with ever since. I can hear their voices, their foreign, familiar language. It may be what draws me to Spain.

I met the trickster in my mother very directly. I'm not talking about some mischievous little imp, though that is part of it too. I'm talking about the dangerous spirit that holds both destruction and creativity. As a teenager, I had argued with her in the backyard, probably something to do with hoeing the garden. I refused to work, then ran inside, locking the side door behind me. Thinking she'd be running to the front to get in there, I raced to lock that door too, then returned to the side door. There she stood, staring through the screen. He face was cold; her blue eyes stared through me. I quietly opened the door. She walked by, not seeing me, not acknowledging my presence. At that moment I was nonexistent, utterly abandoned, and I'd earned my abandonment. Now, I realize, I encountered what Lorca would have called *duende*, face to face. The coldness was a momentary death to a young boy, but it also opened my eyes to the reality of the human soul; it is unknowable. There is something larger than the family's intimacy; each of us, no matter what the community shapes, is alone in the vastness. I won't forget it.

I encountered this *duende* once more in her. This time, though, it was hard to tell who was abandoning whom. When my mother was in her early eighties, my siblings entered her name in a list for vacancies at a home for the aged. They knew the name wouldn't show up for years, so there was time yet for Mother to live in her house. And she did, living independently, driving wherever she needed to go. Her favourite places being her land in the country and the nearby tracks to listen to the trains pass by.

But inevitably her age was taking its toll, and when her name came up a decision had to be made immediately, would she move or not. No one had talked to her about it since her name had first gone onto the list five years previously. We exchanged many emails and phone calls trying to come up with a decision. We knew if we asked Mother she'd refuse to move. So, did we have a right to make a decision for her? We all agreed her life was getting more difficult, and wondered if she could wait another five years if her name went back to the bottom of the list. That would make her ninety-two. Just hours before the deadline we reached a consensus and we told the home we'd accept the suite.

I think my siblings were all somewhat cowed by the prospect of talking to her about this great transition. As the eldest child, I was called in to break the news. I knew this would be a tough conversation. In essence, I felt I was betraying her and taking away some of her freedom. So, was I abandoning my mother? Did I have a right to do that?

I showed up and sat down with her. I waited through a few minutes of small talk before I told her what we had decided. Whatever difficulties I was expecting were nothing compared to what I got. She pretended not to hear what I was saying. She diverted my attention to different things in the room. What did I think of a certain photo on the wall? Had I read the book on the coffee table? I kept bringing her back to the subject, insisting that she look at me. When she did, it was that same blue-eyed stare I'd encountered many decades earlier, though it came from a different place. This time I found myself looking at the cold eyes of a very angry ten-year-old girl. Not a shouting anger, rather a still, focused inner rage. And, as that time long ago, she looked through me. Well, who was abandoning whom?

I had nothing but memories and a crazy present at that point. The ten-year-old stare I was getting was someone I didn't know. What I did remember was the young mother she had been. I remember being in grade five and parents sitting in the classroom for visiting days. Someone told me my mother was a good-looking woman. I hadn't thought of that before. I looked at her, thirty years old, slender with blonde hair, wearing high-heeled shoes, sitting amongst slightly older women who were already dressing in old women's clothes. That was a feature at the time within the religion; one had to look one's age, whatever that meant. One couldn't dress to attract attention.

There had to be not only physical modesty, but a modesty of ego. Mother would be asked occasionally to sing during one church service or another. This was high risk; it was better not to accept the spotlight, better to sing in a choir. But, sometimes, she did. I still have an old 78 recording of her singing "O Holy City" in some one-room studio on Portage Avenue in Winnipeg. She has told me I was less than a year old, my father holding me as she sang. She would have been twenty-one, and it would have been 1947.

But that young mother was now eighty-seven. We were different people. In the moment, she was someone from before my birth. I felt that I could be batted away with one swipe. For a few minutes I didn't exist. I was not her child. I had betrayed her, so why should she see me as her son?

I have some iron in me though. In fact, I held my own anger. I was angry at her recalcitrance. If she'd simply refused to consider moving to the suite, I would have understood, but her refusal even to recognize that I was speaking to her, that I was having my own difficulty in being the messenger of bad news, that angered me. When I tried to engage her in a discussion of the situation, she clammed up: "You'll do whatever you're going to do."

I kept steering her attention back to what I was saying about the need to move. At one point, in reaction to something I said, she blurted out, "I give a rip." I almost laughed. She'd never said that before. It was something I could have said in my teens when I argued with her. I began to see some humour in the situation. How both of us were banging around inside ourselves, from one age to another, trying to react to each other's different people. The boy in me, the girl in her, the adult in both of us. Looking for some solid ground to stand on.

She was the dangerous imp, and I was what? I wasn't the child, and I wasn't the teenager. With a capacity I didn't know was there, I shifted from adult son to messenger to startled adult and back again. At this moment I understood that my childhood was more or less my own private preserve, something I no longer shared with my mother. That was gone. I had abandoned her a long time ago by hiving my life away from hers, from the religious community, growing into my own being. Religion had always inserted itself between us, and I had learned to be wary, not to be too open. There was no little boy sitting in front of her. There was a sadness in this for me. I was acting out an adult responsibility I didn't fully believe in. It was something expected of me. Freedom was so important, always. My freedom, then my children's freedom, and now my mother's. She had a strong need for independence. Yet, there was this day, this moment.

Death is an easier inevitability in a way; it's outside one's control. Ultimately there is no decision to make. One dies. It is the decisions before death that are impossible. Here one runs into what ethicists have called "conflicting sorrows." And I'd expand that with "conflicting freedoms." Whose freedom takes precedence? What is the greater sorrow? If, in fact, freedom is not totally an illusion, it is true that one steadily loses freedom with age. And there is pathos in this balancing act of individual freedom with family responsibility. The back and forth between youth and age. The one who once made decisions for her children, now is in her children's hands. And she is utterly unique, alone in the end.

My mother is fierce, the fire inside her burns intensely. She says she could have kicked the doctor who was responsible for her losing her driver's license. She told me she didn't give a rip about something I was saying. She gave me the blue eye. And, being her son, I gave her the blue eye back. She backed off, saying, "What are you thinking? Are you disgusted with me?" I said that I was disgusted at her refusal to listen, though I understood why she didn't want to lose her independence. At that point it felt like a contest of wills, and I was convinced I couldn't lose this one. I was sure of what had to be done, and I was unsure.

The encounter ended. I wasn't at all certain that the reality of what I had presented had lodged itself in her mind; she still seemed to be in denial. But it was all I could do. We went to the living room, looked at some family photos, and talked of other things. She told me a story about her grandmother, Anna, who was a pivotal figure in my own life. She was as close as I came to a muse in my writing. This old woman, because of events in her early life, and her reactions to those events, had given me permission to be an artist, whatever form it took. There was no other way of understanding life, of living it as fearlessly as possible, not caring about the community's judgment.

Later that evening, with my siblings and their partners, we met at a restaurant. I sat beside my mother. My family is loquacious, conversations were flying across the table. As I was listening to my youngest sister, I became aware that my mother had her hand on my head. She was gently ruffling what is left of my hair. Then her hand moved to my shoulder. I thought she was forgiving me. Or she was saying she was sorry. I don't know which, or was it both? In her fierce love of independence, and in her love for me, she was saying she understood what I had done that day, and it was okay.

My young mother, with a child's heart beating. The child that has never abandoned her through marriage, childbirth, her sometimes-difficult children, the loss of her husband, and all the vagaries of a long life. The imp, mischievous always with tricks, with the turnarounds of language, the imp who is dangerous, the imp has become almost helpless. Mother says sometimes that she is shocked when she hears how old she is. As far as she knows she was ten or eleven just yesterday. And she was.

Contributors

HOWARD DYCK was born in Winkler, Manitoba, and currently resides in Waterloo, Ontario. He is conductor of the Nota Bene Baroque Players & Singers, artistic director emeritus of the Grand Philharmonic Choir (Kitchener-Waterloo), and conductor emeritus of the Bach Elgar Choir (Hamilton). His international conducting career has taken him to twenty countries on three continents. He is well-known across Canada as the former host of *Choral Concert* and *Saturday Afternoon at the Opera* on CBC Radio. He is a Member of the Order of Canada and a recipient of the Queen's Golden and Diamond Jubilee Medals.

CHRISTOFF ENGBRECHT was born in Winnipeg, Manitoba, and has lived there for most of his life. Over the past decade his poems have been published by several Canadian poetry journals, including *CV2* and *Prairie Fire*.

PATRICK FRIESEN was born in Steinbach, Manitoba, spent most of his life in Winnipeg, and now lives with his wife, Eve, in Victoria. He teaches one course in the Writing Department at the University of Victoria. He has just published a long poem called "a short history of crazy bone," and is working on a trio of plays and a poetry manuscript.

142 Contributors

MICHAEL GOERTZEN was born in Chilliwack, British Columbia, in 1976. He graduated with an English literature degree from the University of Winnipeg. He currently teaches English language arts at a middle school in Turkey. His writing has appeared in various literary publications, including *Grain Magazine*, *Poetry is Dead*, and *Palaspandıras Fanzin*.

NATHAN KLIPPENSTEIN was born in Goshen, Indiana, while his father was studying there. He has lived in Winnipeg for most of his life, with a few teaching stints in Belize, Japan, and Mexico City. He has been living and working in Winnipeg for about twenty years and has found, particularly through this writing piece, that teaching writing and grammar to junior high school students can be easier than writing something yourself.

MARY ANN LOEWEN was born in Lincoln, Nebraska, but has lived most of her life in Manitoba. She worked as a nurse in her twenties, taught piano in her thirties and forties, and then discovered an interest in English literature and writing. She has previously published several pieces on the topic of Mennonite mothers and daughters. Currently she teaches Academic Writing at the University of Winnipeg. She loves to write, to run, and to work in the kitchen; she is married and has three lovely grown children.

ANDREW C. MARTIN was born in Kitchener, Ontario, and currently lives in nearby Elmira. He is a part-time counselling therapist while working on a doctoral dissertation at Toronto School of Theology, University of Toronto. His research project traces ascetical and mystical spiritual themes from medieval monasticism to define and demonstrate the spirituality of Old Order Mennonites. He has published in several academic journals on Anabaptist-Mennonite history, theology, and spirituality.

JOSIAH NEUFELD was born in Kamsack, Saskatchewan, but spent most of his growing-up years in Burkina Faso. He is a writer and freelance journalist who now lives in Winnipeg. His fiction, essays, and long-form journalism have been published in *The Walrus*, *Prairie Fire*, *The New Quarterly*, *The Globe & Mail*, and *Geez*. In 2014 he received the Dave Greber Freelance Writers Award for social justice writing. He is currently working on a novel.

LLOYD RATZLAFF is the author of three books of literary nonfiction published by Thistledown Press, *The Crow Who Tampered With Time* (2002), *Backwater Mystic Blues* (2006), and *Bindy's Moon* (2015). He has edited an anthology of seniors' writings for READ Saskatoon, and is a long-time columnist for *Prairie Messenger Catholic Journal*. He has served on the boards of several writing organizations and taught writing classes for the University of Saskatchewan Certificate of Art & Design program and the Western Development Museum. He was born in Saskatoon and still lives there.

BYRON REMPEL is the author of *True Detective* (not starring Matthew McConaughey), *Truth is Naked*, an autobiographical exaggeration, and *No Limits*, a twin biography. He has a new, currently homeless novel waiting to burst forth upon the world. Byron grew up in Steinbach, Manitoba, and currently divides his time between the Quebec Laurentians and Florida scrublands.

JOHN REMPEL was born in Waterloo, Ontario in 1944. He studied theology in Elkhart (Indiana), Berlin, and Toronto. He has been a pastor, Mennonite Central Committee worker, and professor of theology. Now in semi-retirement, he is the director of the Toronto Mennonite Theological Centre.

LUKAS THIESSEN holds a BA from Canadian Mennonite University, as well as a BA Honours in History and an MA in Cultural Studies from the University of Winnipeg. He has worked as a research assistant for various professors on topics related to Mennonite history and culture, has recently studied Low German, is a public speaker on topics related to the intersections of religious culture and atheism, and recently contributed an article to the *Journal of Mennonite Studies*. He also works in the field of art history as a research assistant, tour guide, and volunteer, and provides assistance with the development of new media for exhibitions. He was born, and currently resides, in Winnipeg.

Contributors

PAUL TIESSEN was born in 1944 in Kitchener, Ontario. He is professor emeritus of English and Film Studies at Wilfrid Laurier University in Waterloo, Ontario, where he taught from 1974 to 2011. He has publishing projects underway on novelist Malcolm Lowry, media theorist Marshall McLuhan, and Mennonite writers including Rudy Wiebe and Miriam Toews. He and his wife, Hildi Froese Tiessen, live in Kitchener.